Simply God

A Tutorial in Receiving All God Has to Offer

CHARLES L. SPENCER

WESTBOW°
PRESS
A DIVISION OF THOMAS NELSON
& ZONDERVAN

WestBow Press books may be ordered through booksellers or by contacting:

WestBow Press
A Division of Thomas Nelson & Zondervan
1663 Liberty Drive
Bloomington, IN 47403
www.westbowpress.com
1 (866) 928-1240

ISBN: 978-1-4908-3830-4 (sc)
ISBN: 978-1-4908-3829-8 (hc)
ISBN: 978-1-4908-3831-1 (e)

Library of Congress Control Number: 2014909430

Printed in the United States of America.

WestBow Press rev. date: 06/03/2014

Contents

Acknowledgments vii

Prologue ix

Chapter 1: Simply God 1

Chapter 2: The Great Commission 7

Chapter 3: Why 20

Chapter 4: How 28

Chapter 5: The "What Now?" 31

Chapter 6: A Holy Spirit 43

Chapter 7: It's Not All Good 51

Chapter 8: The Holy Wow 59

Chapter 9: The Purpose 72

Chapter 10: Anyone Seen My Body? 83

Chapter 11: The Evil Empire 89

Chapter 12: Our Kingdom 96

Chapter 13: Counterfeit 105

Chapter 14: Secrets 112

Chapter 15: The Theist 118

Chapter 16: Holiness 126

Chapter 17: Blocking the Benefits 139

Chapter 18: Prosperity 148

Chapter 19: Give and It Shall Be Given 155

Chapter 20: The Ways and Means of Giving 166

Chapter 21: My Ordeal 178

Chapter 22: Health... 187

Chapter 23: Healed 194

Chapter 24: Wear Good Shoes 208

Chapter 25: That's All, Folks.. 214

Acknowledgments

It took me a while to write this book. I grew tired along the way. I had moments of insecurity and doubt. There are a few people that kept me moving forward and who inspired me on this journey. First, my wife. We started out in marriage at 17 and have literally grown up together. She has stood by my side for the last 50 years and I am so grateful for her support. Thank you to my son and daughter who were so encouraging and helpful whenever I needed it.

Thank you to my grandchildren who just by being give me a reason to try to be my best self and gave me the inspiration to want to leave something that will exist long after I have gone.

Thank you also to my fellowship whose prayers keep me going and all of my friends who for the last 40 years have inspired me. Also, those who through their love, patience and understanding helped me to heal and mature. I am sorry I can not name you but you know who you are and I hope you know how much you have meant to me and how much I appreciate you.

Lastly, but in all ways, first, thank you to God. I believe God loves literature. He loves His word. He has inspired authors as long as time has existed. This book was inspired by the Holy Spirit and was completed because of the dogged determination of the Holy Spirit. 100 times I gave up and 100 times the Holy Spirit took me back to my computer. Knowing this, I thank the God of this completed project. On my own, I complete very little. Through Him, I have completed much.

Prologue

I am nearly finished with this book, and as is my habit, I have reviewed what I have written over a two-year period. As I reviewed some of the material in this book, I realized much of it makes me sound like an overbearing, judgmental, pompous jerk, and I must confess, the reason for that is quite simple. Much of the time I am an opinionated, overbearing, judgmental, pompous jerk. In his book _Satan's Dirty Little Secret,_ Steve Foss (Creation House, Lake Mary, Florida 2007) contends that two principal demons of Satan are insecurity and inferiority (page 10). I further realized that much of this book could foster feelings of inferiority if not also insecurity. This is absolutely not what I intended. In fact, I must make a confession. In this book I talk a great deal about faith, inadvertently leaving the impression I have a good handle on it. That is not true. In most areas my faith is inferior to that of many of the people around me. But I take great hope in this knowledge, combined with the knowledge that God's promises are all true. Knowing the truth of God's Word, I will keep practicing until my faith through the Holy Spirit becomes mature.

If I was a bull rider in the rodeo, I would have to express my life since beginning to write this book as having been thrown, stomped, butted, and gored and all of that without even going the eight seconds. It seems to me that maybe even the clown kicked me.

Two things have stimulated by mind down this present path. One was the vehement attack that my person has been under, and the second was the unanimous belief of my immediate fellowship that

I was under attack from the Devil and that he was trying to kill me to stop me from pursuing the theology outlined in this thesis. I do not believe the Evil One has any new tricks, but history can teach us how he uses his old tried-and-true devices. I looked at the preachers of faith and healing to see if I could find a pattern. I believe without great effort that I did see a definite pattern. Now please do not misunderstand me. When I name the names I name, I am not comparing myself with their revelations or ministries. I will confess that for most of my life on their worst day and my best day I would not make a pimple on their posterior. But I do take comfort in the fact that I am going through trials similar to what many of them went through.

There's no way I could call my study of this demonic phenomenon extensive, but it was extremely interesting, and I encourage you to study the modern forerunners of faith theology. **"The thief comes only to steal and kill and destroy; I have come that they may have life, and have it to the full" (John 10:10).** Not only did I see a pattern as I looked into twentieth-century faith healers, but the pattern was somewhat involved with the above Scripture.

A good example of this pattern was John Alexander Dowie. Dowie was a controversial, elegant, persuasive speaker who ministered in the United States from the late 1800s to the early 1900s. Around 1900, he was successful enough to buy a large chunk of land in northern Illinois and establish the city of Zion. Zion, Illinois, was supposed to be a Mecca of holiness, not allowing smoking, drinking, the eating of pork, or the establishment of theaters, dance halls, doctors' surgeries, and secret lodges. Mr. Dowie found himself constantly in trouble with the civilian authorities for practicing medicine without a license, and in 1895 spent some time in jail for the same. While he was defending himself in court, his second-in-charge hijacked his ministry, and while Mr. Dowie litigated to get it back, he was unsuccessful. A number of unsubstantiated allegations of misuse of funds and sexual misconduct were slung about, ruining his reputation, and within two years he was dead, never having reached the age of sixty.

Another example of a ruined ministry using the same tactics was that of Jack Cole. I am not denying that these ministers were controversial and had some contrary ideas, but so did Jesus. Jack Cole was a post–World War II faith healer with the biggest tent in the world. Through much of his ministry, Cole was hounded by civilian authorities for practicing medicine without a license. In fact, he was arrested in Florida for telling the parents of a small boy with polio that he was cured and that they should remove his leg braces. According to records, this caused the boy a great deal of pain, and he eventually died of polio. The charges against Cole were dismissed by a judge because of a technicality. Cole was also thrown out of the Assemblies of God, basically because he was not a strong supporter of organized religion and also because he caused civil authorities discomfort. He was also charged by denominational authorities for living too extravagant a lifestyle, even though his home was smaller than that of several leaders in the Assemblies of God. As with many of the faith healers of the twentieth century, Jack Cole did not reach the age of sixty. Ironically, he died of complications from polio.

So here's the Devil's pattern: depending on what the individual preaches, the Devil will form an unholy alliance to attack his or her body, theology, and integrity. The unholy alliance is between civil authorities (practicing medicine without a license), organized religion, and the press. He gets the preachers so busy defending themselves that he literally steals their time for ministry. The stress is so great that their bodies begin to break down, and often they die. I never fully understood the Scripture John 10:10, for it says the Devil came to kill and destroy. That seems redundant to me, for if you kill somebody, don't you destroy them? In researching this demonic phenomenon of attacking faith preachers, I came to realize that although the Devil may kill them, he also needs to destroy their testimony. To do this, he uses allegations of sexual misconduct and/ or financial misconduct. He employs the press to sensationalize and overstate the truth. To me the most distressing element of this unholy alliance is when the Evil One uses organized religion to attack their own. And it is so easy: we will throw anyone under the bus who does not agree with our dogmatic narrow-mindedness.

Here is a list of twentieth-century faith preachers who never reached the age of sixty: Dorothea Trudell, William Branhan, Jack Cole and both men who are usually credited with the Azusa Street revivals, William Joseph Seymour, and Charles Fox Parham. What most of them had in common was that they believed in faith healing and had conflicts with organized religion.

It would seem to me from the minimal research I have done that destroying our testimony is very important to the Devil, for it seems it is what he has tried to do almost universally to all faith preachers: Aimee McPherson, Kathryn Kuhlman, Oral Roberts—the list could go on and on. One mistake and their reputations are splattered across the front pages.

With the emergence of prosperity gospel, more and more emphasis is put on the misappropriation of funds by evangelists. Mostly, it just talks about how much they have. This is a little hard for me to understand, because basically there are two approaches to the prosperity gospel. One is tithing, a principle I will talk about later and do not believe in. Tithing made simple is that you give 10 percent of your income to God and in return, God makes a promise. **"'Test me in this,' says the Lord Almighty, 'and see if I will not throw open the floodgates of heaven and pour out so much blessing that you will not have room enough for it'" (Malachi 3:10).** Okay, here's the rub: if I fulfill the tithe, God says I will not have room enough for what he returns to me. Then I am criticized for all I have, and even if I give away most of it, God says he will give me more. Suddenly I find myself with a $60 million surplus and spending thirty-five hours a week in commercial airports waiting in line, so it only makes sense to buy a jet. Then I am further criticized because I own a jet. The implication is that I am improperly using donor dollars to create a lavish lifestyle. The God element is eliminated. (Please understand that the *I* of the above illustration is purely hypothetical. I do not own a jet.)

The other principle of prosperity is called sowing and reaping, which is a principle I do believe in and was popularized by Oral Roberts. The principle is basically the same; God says that as you sow, so shall you reap. In other words, if I give away a lot, God returns a lot to me, and the same merry-go-round begins, exposing the preacher to criticism. Rarely does anyone who is doing the criticizing look at what the preacher has given away. They look only at his lifestyle. And never are the words of Jesus quoted: "I have come that you may have life and have it abundantly."

Please bear with me as I tell one more story of an evangelist and faith healer who spectacularly fell from grace. I'm fairly familiar with this story. One reason is that he and his TV programs were my introduction to faith healing; I watched when I was a child. Furthermore, when the story unfolded, my daughter was a freshman at Oral Roberts University on a full scholarship. Of course, the man I'm speaking of is Oral Roberts. Mr. Roberts had not had an easy life to this point and paid a lot in emotional loss to gain his ministry, which included an accredited university. Mr. Roberts felt God was telling him to build a hospital, which would be a prayer center for the ill and infirm. I will not say I condoned his method, however, these many years later, the national medias attentions to his methods seems like overkill. My daughter even to this day would describe it with emotion in her voice as very distracting. She speaks of walking out of classes and having a reporter from a national news network sticking a microphone in students' faces and asking them leading questions about Mr. Roberts, a man they all loved and respected. After that year, my daughter did not return to ORU, saying she wanted an education and was afraid that her diploma would have a stain on it from the media circus attacking the university. Why the national media was so interested in Oral Roberts going into his prayer tower and declaring that God said he would die if he did not get the money for the City of Faith was and is beyond me. With all the national media attention, his donations dried up, and the hospital to this day is an empty shell. Oral retired and died a somewhat broken, unfulfilled man. The university suffered greatly without his leadership. These many years later, my daughter still speaks kindly of the sweet old man who would greet students on the campus as if they were members of his family.

If you read chapter 21, called "My Ordeal," you will understand why I felt I needed to write this prologue. I spoke earlier of the Devil destroying our testimony; certainly, he can do that by putting a stain on our character and muddying our integrity. But another way is like he almost did with me: attacking me in such a way that he almost made me doubt my own testimony.

CHAPTER 1

Simply God

Man seems to have a fatal flaw, which is the necessity to complicate that which is simple. Historically, God's dealings with man have been quite straightforward. He said what he meant, and he meant what he said. But we always want to believe there is more, as if God is withholding something from us and our lives will be better if we discover it. The truth of the matter is, we want to hear God in human form, and as one of the great Bible teachers, Dr. Mark Rutland, says, we must speak God to understand God. I have found we do not speak God by understanding; rather, we speak God by believing.

Take Adam and Eve, for instance. God placed them in the garden with a few simple instructions, and they frolicked in naked innocence until the Evil One began to make them think instead of believe. Although there is a great deal to learn from the story of the garden, my point is that God is not interested in our knowing *about* him. Rather he wants us to know him and, in that knowing, believe him. It is the Evil One who wants us forever learning and never coming to knowledge of the truth (2 Timothy 3:7). It is not even enough to believe in him, for we could believe that he existed, that he was a man of peace, even the Son of God. We could go to church every Sunday because of him and know that if we only obeyed him, our lives would be better and yet see our lives little different from that of our neighbors who ignore him completely. It is only as we believe his preposterous claims that we find ourselves changed into "new creatures" (2 Corinthians 5:17). It is these claims that we intend to explore and this believing we hope to have kindled.

Jesus did not give us a philosophy of life. He gave us life. He did not come that we should think; he came that we should be. He did not ask us to consider; he called us to believe. Jesus was quite straightforward in what he said to his disciples, that as we begin to believe to receive, the eyes of our hearts will be enlightened in order that **we may know the hope to which he has called us, the riches of his glorious inheritance in the saints (Ephesians 1:18).**

Adam and Eve were not the only example of this error of complication. It is prevalent throughout the biblical history of man. Take for instance the case of Abraham. Abram was a man called by God, who promised him that not only would he be blessed, but he would be a blessing. Certainly implied within this blessing was provision of every kind, including substance and protection. The blessing seems quite simple and straightforward, yet when faced with famine in the land, Abram fled to Egypt.

In a biblical context, Egypt is never a place for God's people. While in Egypt, as is always the case when God's people are in the wrong place, Abram became afraid. But true to his word, God rescued him. Sometime after this, God again spoke to Abram and made his word even plainer. He said, "Do not be afraid, Abram. I am your shield, your very great reward." And at this point, the journey from Abram to Abraham begins, for if *Abram* means "one who was called," *Abraham* means "one who believes the calling." It is not the calling that makes us righteous. It is the believing. In Genesis 12, Abram was called, but it was not till Genesis 15 that he was chosen. It was not the call that changed him but the believing. "Abram believed the Lord, and it was credited to him as righteousness" (Genesis 15:6).

As Abram became Abraham, he continued to struggle. But God continued to be faithful to his word, and Abraham, as he watched the faithfulness of God, learned to be faithful to believing.

Let me give one more example of complicating the simplicity of God. The Israelites were stuck in Egypt (there we go again in Egypt), and God delivered them. They had no God structure, no constitution, no laws, and no idea how to live as a group of free people. God intervened and gave them ten simple rules that would keep them at peace with him, each other, and themselves. They, however, could not trust the simplicity of God and almost immediately and for several centuries developed a set of religious rules that controlled every area of their lives. Yet these man-made rules actually separated them from God, their neighbors, and even themselves. As an interesting aside, God's rules will always unite, whereas man's rules will always divide. Whenever man adds to God's rules, they become divisive.

So there it is! It is not our intellect, calling, or religious rules that make an impression upon God. Only our believing does.

I had a troubled childhood that lasted into my forties. The reason it took me so long to begin the maturation process was that my childhood made me suspicious, insecure, and defensive. I found trusting nearly impossible. I questioned everything, looked for hidden motives everywhere, and consequently complicated life.

I believe it was this propensity to complicate that led me to the revelation of God's simplicity. He patiently worked with me over many years to bring me to this point in life. Whenever I would complicate things and think that God had hidden motives, he would bring me back to the same place. He would take my complicated theology and simplify it until I got a picture of a God I could understand and trust.

When I began to put the pieces of the puzzle together, I found there were simply five principles of God at work in my life—five principles that when put together, trusted, and believed give me life and life abundant. However, I need to clarify something here. You can read this book and understand and intellectually believe everything in it, but if you do not allow the Holy Spirit to bring forth these victorious truths in your life, you will have achieved nothing. These great promises of God are meant to be life changing.

The five principles of God, when believed, become life-changing experiences. These principles are simply his gifts to us. We do nothing but believe to receive. The five are an exchanged life, a whole spirit, a healed body, a prosperous soul, and a godly character.

This volume is not intended to add to the endless words about who God is, what he wants, and what our purpose is. Our goal is to, as simply as possible, use the Word of God to show that through Jesus Christ, the Father has provided us with all things (2 Corinthians 9:8), and our purpose is to simply believe the unbelievable. Even this believing is not of ourselves but a gift from him (Hebrews 12:2). So consider this: if Jesus is the author and perfecter of our faith (that is, our belief), the only thing that would keep us from receiving all his promises is our choice not to believe.

Some of the men I fellowship with and I went to a retreat (the sponsors called it an advance). One of the presenters had a unique gift. As he was teaching, he would quote appropriate Scripture so fast from memory that one could hardly keep up. The substance of his seminar, however, taught us very little that the Holy Spirit had not already revealed to us as a group. The substance of his teaching impressed us little, but his gift of the knowledge of Scripture subsequently stimulated more conversation than all of the seminars combined. The younger men in the Lord were very impressed, but the older men declared it little more than a parlor trick if it was not mixed with faith. I personally believe the presenter was a man of faith who mixed the Word with faith.

As the discussion progressed, it became obvious that the younger men were judging the presenter's spirituality by his giftedness and judging their own spirituality by comparing his giftedness with what they thought was their lack of it. The older men in the group, on the other hand, declared that giftedness has nothing to do with spirituality. For example, you do not call a man a good businessman because he has inherited a million dollars. He has simply been given a gift. You determine a man's spirituality by the way he treats his wife in private and how he handles himself in relationship to the world. This is a great mistake the church often makes in following a man because of his gifts and knowing little or nothing of his character. But that is not my point in telling this story.

As the discussion progressed, and its nature became obvious, one of the men summed himself up like this: "I may not be able to always quote the appropriate Word of God, but I always know and believe the principles of God." And that is what this book is about: knowing and believing the principles of God. Now don't get me wrong. I believe in reading and knowing the Word, but I stand by the statement that it is more important to know and believe the principles of God than it is to know the Word of God. People read the Word of God every day and yet never apply it to life.

Now let's talk about application. We in the West think in a very Greco-Roman manner. That is, we want to understand a matter and be able to philosophize about it. We tend to be thinkers. To us, the most important thing is to know the meaning of something. Because of the interpretation of the Bible from this Roman-Greco mind-set combined with centuries of political tension, the church has strayed far from the simple truth of God.

However, the Bible was written from an Eastern mind-set. The question this mind-set asks is not "What does it mean?" but rather "How do I believe?" This mind-set does not seek to understand what something means but rather its application to life.

That is exactly what this book is about: the application of knowing the hope of this great calling of ours, this glorious inheritance, which can never be understood just received by faith. It is far too richly glorious for us to truly understand with our carnal minds. And this book is about glory, his glory shared with us, about us enjoying it for a moment and then the victory as we give it back to him. That is so different from the beginning, when Adam and Eve reached for the glory of being like God and held it for themselves. We need not take it, for it is His gift to us. Our gift to him is to be a living demonstration of this glory to a lost and dying world.

CHAPTER 2

The Great Commission

"**Therefore go and make disciples of all nations, baptizing them in the name of the Father and Son and Holy Spirit and teaching them to do everything that I have commanded you" (Matthew 28:19).** This Scripture is often referred to as the Great Commission. What is this Great Commission (not a term found in the Bible), this great calling of God, and this central theme of the Bible? Is it truly, as many believe, all about getting people to heaven when they die?

I had a friend who believed this and lived his life dedicated to getting people to proclaim certain beliefs that assured them of heaven when they died. I was with him at the moment his spirit left his body, and in the last hours of his life on earth, his proclamation was "The Bible says a lot about living but precious little about dying." As I thought about this statement, it began to make sense to me. The Bible is a book written to the living about living.

Much emphasis is put upon receiving Jesus Christ as our personal Savior and going to heaven when we die. That is what I referred to as saying the magic words. I believe this easy gospel began about the turn of the last century and could not be further from the true gospel. This gospel, when combined with the doctrine of once saved always saved, is the Devil's plan of damnation. It lulls people into a sort of spiritual coma, from which many never awake. We are told to be hot or cold but that if we are lukewarm, we shall be spit out of his mouth. This mentality of a brief encounter and convincing someone that if they say certain words and then maybe do certain things, they will go to heaven when they die, falls very short of the true core message of the Bible.

I realize of course that this line of thinking is very contrary to the accepted theology of most evangelicals and that many of the readers of this book will at this point consider me mistaken at best or a heretic at worst. But to those who will maintain an open mind and press on, I believe I can show you quite easily from the biblical record a better way.

Now do not misunderstand me, I don't mean a better way from the divine perspective. The Father's plan is perfect. In a word it is Jesus. Jesus is the only way of life everlasting. **John 14:6 says, "Jesus answered, 'I am the way and the truth and the life. No one comes to the Father except through me.'"**

It cannot be said any simpler that Jesus has given us the only way of eternal life (**"to bring eternal life through Jesus Christ Our Lord" [(Rom. 5:21]).** Eternity begins the moment we truly accept Jesus Christ as our Lord and Savior. When he says I am the way, the truth, and the life, he means in this life now and forever more. It is not a promise for when we die. It is the human delivery system and the human expectations—or rather, the lack of them— that I question.

Maybe we can gain some insight by taking a closer look at the Scripture that started this chapter. Is this Scripture telling us what we think it is, or is it telling us that the most important thing is not to get somebody "saved" but rather to make them disciples and to teach them everything that Jesus taught his disciples? We can certainly see that it directs us to baptize them, and that is something that takes a certain amount of time and preparation. Consider the Lord's Prayer, in which Jesus asks the Father that the kingdom come and that the Father's will be done on earth as it is in heaven. Maybe God's true purpose is to make kingdom disciples.

Several years ago I had an experience that changed my way of thinking forever. As I realized that what I had been taught was wrong, it opened my spirit up for the Holy Spirit to show me the true meaning of evangelism.

I received a phone call one evening in late summer from a friend. He told me of a man standing on a corner destitute, hungry, and homeless. My friend felt a need to help this man but said he could not take the man home, for his wife would not approve. I said, "Bring him to my house, and we will care for him." When they arrived, I proceeded to tell the traveler that no matter how he answered my questions, he would be provided with new clothes, a meal, and a warm bed. I then proceeded to walk him through the five spiritual laws. About halfway through my brilliant presentation, he interrupted me and asked me if I was referring to the sinner's prayer. I answered him yes, and he proceeded to tell me he had already proclaimed the sinner's prayer six or seven times in his life. This man's life was completely out of control. He was alcoholic, demon possessed, and completely self-destructive. He was perhaps my age and looked to be ten to fifteen years older. Was he going to heaven when he died, which was not too far down the road he was then on? I simply do not know, but one thing I did know was that his life was filled with death and defeat. This sinner's prayer, which he had so willingly repeated so many times, had done nothing to set him free from his demons in this life.

This evangelism of an easy gospel is carried on for the most part by people who feel compelled on a soul level to be doing something for God. I truly understand this compulsion; we are the generation that was raised believing there is no free lunch. We were raised to believe that if you worked hard, you got rewarded. Therefore, when it comes to God, it is hard for us to believe there is nothing we can do to get him to love us more. We need not and in fact cannot earn his love; Jesus provided all that is needed to receive all the Father has. I believe the church must be evangelistic in nature, but when we are driven by this mandate evangelism, it smacks of misunderstanding the nature of the triune God. It fails to understand that the Father's love is consistent and does not depend upon our actions, good or bad. It fails to understand the absolute completed work of Jesus Christ, when he said, "It is finished" and then later sat down at the right hand of the Father. Work was finished, and anything I try to add outside the leading of the Holy Spirit is filthy rags. And of course this leading of the Holy Spirit is the paramount thing. When I believe I have a blanket obligation to verbally testify to everyone I meet, I simply deny the Lordship of the Holy Spirit in my life. The belief that someone is obligated to testify is in my opinion, as nefarious as a Christian's hesitation or fear to testify.

This compulsion for evangelism is prevalent among certain elements of the church, and yours truly must confess he was once a votary. When I consider those I have known who are overtly evangelistic, two men come to mind. I am hesitant to be very outspoken about their actions because they are both excellent friends; in fact, outside of my immediate core group, these two men are perhaps the only ones who I know always have my back. These two men, although from very different backgrounds, have many things in common. Both are extremely successful in their business endeavors and work very hard. Both are very loyal to their friends and have few enemies. And both, in spite of their huge professional successes, do not seem satisfied with who they are and what they have accomplished. Both these fine gentlemen seem quite pensive about their relationship with God. There seems to be a need to continually prove themselves before men. This need convinces me that they do not have a complete understanding that, no matter the past, in Jesus Christ the Father God completely approves of them. Any human need that has not been healed by God makes us *driven* and therefore does not allow us to be *led* by the Holy Spirit.

It is a very easy thing to get people to say the magic words when all that is involved is their going to heaven when they die. However, it becomes much harder for both parties when you speak of the death to self and commit yourself to teaching them how to walk in that death.

Many years ago I had a brief experience of evangelizing in Nepal. Nepal is primarily a Hindu country. I had absolutely no problem drawing large crowds at any street corner, and at first many would accept my invitation to receive Jesus Christ as their personal Savior. Then I suddenly realized they did not mind at all accepting another god to add to their "300 million gods." After that, I explained in my message that this God was a jealous God and would not accept them worshipping any other God but him. My number of converts dropped considerably.

I think the same might happen in America if it was explained that if you are going to be a Christian, you must die to self. Not only must you die to self, but self will disappear into something much greater called the body of Christ, where individualism will be lost.

In his fine book on spiritual deliverance *Shadow Boxing,* Henry Malone (Vision Life, Irving,Texas 1999) speaks of an occult conspiracy that actually puts satanic worshippers in churches as teachers to get people to believe this easy gospel of accepting Jesus Christ as your Lord and Savior so you can go to heaven and yet expects no change here and now. There is no real born-again experience .They are led to make an intellectual assent to the gospel but no spiritual commitment (Chapter 9 page 140-141).. **"Jesus answered, 'I tell you the truth,**

no one can enter the kingdom of God unless he is born of water and the Spirit. Flesh gives birth to flesh, but the Spirit gives birth to spirit'" (John 3:5–6).

There is probably no part of this good news of Jesus Christ that has been more understated and misstated than this salvation message. The first part of the misunderstanding comes from considering that we have anything to do with accepting Jesus Christ. We do not. **So, too, at the present time there is a remnant chosen by grace (Romans 11:5).** There are two words present in this Scripture that are significant. Romans 11:5 clearly points to the fact that we are chosen. It clearly points in the direction of God's choice of us and not our choosing of him. But the more important word in the Scripture is *grace.*

Grace defined is "unmerited favor." We have done nothing to deserve God's attention to our lives; it is simply his nature to bless us. Grace understood is our greatest insight into the true character of God. He above all is a giver and withholds nothing from us if we only believe. We are all familiar with John 3:16 as the Scripture key to the normal salvation message. However, if we just look at the first part of that Scripture, we may begin to understand more closely the true nature of God. **John 3:16** says, **"For God so loved the world that he gave ..."** He is not just a giver, but as the Word says, he is a giver of grand proportion. **"He who did not spare his own Son, but gave him up for us all—how will he not also, along with him, graciously give us all things?"** (Romans 8:32).

This trait of God—to give—is so pervasive in his personality that I believe it is predominantly his personality. In fact, we should wonder if we have it all wrong when we say we are to serve God. I believe God created us to have someone to serve. It is certainly the teaching with which Jesus left us: the greatest among you shall be the servant of all. Would anybody argue that God, Father, Son, or Spirit would be the greatest among us? I think it would be easy to see that he serves us so that we have something with which to serve others. Maybe this insistence that we serve God is just egotistical semantics to make us feel more important. God does not particularly need our service; however, humanity could certainly use some help from those who are willing to get their spiritual hands dirty.

Thinking of God as giver is a philosophy we can possibly understand, but the idea of God the servant may be a little harder for us to get our theological grip on. Jesus was not just referring to his walk on earth when he said in **Matthew 20:28, "just as the Son of Man did not come to be served, but to serve."** I think it is a very important for us to understand this extreme giving and serving nature of God to fully understand how we are saved. Basically, he did it all!

Romans 8:30 says, "And those he predestined, he also called; those he called, he also justified; those he justified, he also glorified." Okay, I am having a little trouble understanding what we had to do with this process. Verse 30 says God predestined, called, justified, and glorified. None of this process of salvation seems to leave a lot of room for us or our egos.

When I hear people telling of their experience of leading someone to Christ or even their own salvation experience—that is, being born again on such-and-such a day in such-and-such a way—I immediately suspect they do not know much about the character of God and have made little progress in this rebirth experience. Mostly, these people have a soul need to please people and God.

Let us take the case of Jacob and Esau. The Word says that God hated one and loved the other. **"Just as it is written: 'Jacob I loved, but Esau I hated'" (Romans 9:13).** Okay, let us move by the theological question: what does it mean, "God hates." As far as I

13

can see from looking at the Greek, it means God hated. The more important question is why. Why did God hate Esau and love Jacob?

It was God's choice to love Jacob before he was in the womb, and his choice to hate Esau. This choosing seems to be a characteristic of God that is hard to reconcile with modern evangelical theology. However, the Scriptures are very clear and overwhelmingly convincing when taken at face value: at some time before we existed, God made a choice to accept one and reject another.

"For those God fore knew he also predestined to be ..." (Romans 8:29).

"[H]e predestined us to be adopted" (Ephesians 1:5).

"In him we were also chosen, having been predestined according to the plan of him" (Ephesians 1:11).

... who have been chosen according to the foreknowledge of God the Father" (1 Peter 1:2).

"God, who has called you" (1 Corinthians 1:9).

As you can see, there is a preponderance of evidence that God makes the choices. Okay, I can hear you out there trying to pull me into a Calvinistic-Arminian discussion, and I am not going there for several reasons.

1) It is not what I am talking about.
2) There is no end to that argument.
3) Wesley and Whitfield argued it to a standstill, never reaching a conclusion, and went on to remain friends
4) And finally, I can never remember which is which.

What am I talking about? Simply put, the egocentric modern-day style of evangelism is not effective. This type of evangelism probably started with D. L. Moody near the turn of the twentieth century. Basically, it is speaking to a large group of unrelated people and trying to persuade as many as possible to publicly profess that they are sinners and must repent and accept Jesus Christ as their Savior. Then they will go to heaven when they die. The implication is they need to repent because of their sin. Their habit of sin is not the problem; it is their nature of sin from which they need to be delivered, but more on that later.

It is the unrelatedness of this style of evangelism that makes it unsuccessful. In all the great revivals up to modern times, the evangelist would go to a region and spend a significant amount of time there. He not only saw to people's conversions, but was concerned that they were taught and established, with overseers to look after them. An example is John Wesley and his method, which was so effective not only in bringing about individual change in people's lives but also in changing society around them.

True evangelism should bring about radical change in individuals and ultimately, society. **"We were therefore buried with him through baptism into death in order that, just as Christ was raised from the dead through the glory of the Father, we too may live a new life" (Romans 6:4).**

A friend struggled for years with the gospel. He came from a very liberal family and in our discussions would ridicule conservative ideas. For instance, his family believed abortion was a mother's natural right. After the Holy Spirit opened his spiritual eyes to see the truth of Jesus Christ, he was in a conversation with several family members when someone mentioned abortion. He heard someone say that abortion was just wrong. To the shock of everyone present, including himself, he realized he had said it. He had not formulated a change in his mind; rather, as his spirit became alive within, it brought about a renewal of his mind.

One very large evangelistic ministry has been quoted as saying that after one year, less than 10 percent of their converts were still professing, active Christians. The difference between the examples above of the man whose mind was renewed and the 90 percent who made a commitment and can no longer be found is one word: *expectation.*

The individual whose mind was renewed was told this renewal would happen when he came to accept Jesus Christ as Lord. On the other hand, most evangelical ministries tell people they must admit they are a sinner, repent from their sins, say certain words, and profess their salvation to the person next to them, and then they will go to heaven when they die. They're then told they must do certain things if they are to grow spiritually. Hogwash.

There is absolutely no verifiable evidence that anything has happened to these people except their emotions have been appealed to. The gospel if anything is verifiable. When people truly see Jesus Christ as Lord, they can expect to and will see change. It will come upon them as they expect it, for it is the work of the Holy Spirit. It does not depend upon our works. It is the sovereign work of God. **Hebrews 11:6** <u>says,</u> **"… because anyone who comes to him must believe that he exists and that he rewards those who earnestly seek him."**

As we begin to believe he exists the earnestly seeking him is expecting the reward, the greatest of which is a renewed mind.

Jesus said little about going to heaven, but much about heaven coming to earth. Take the Lord's Prayer, for instance, which says, *"Thy kingdom come, thy will be done on earth."* Could this be our Great

Commission, bringing forth this kingdom upon earth now? *Could it be that the Father is not interested in us living the minimum Christian life to get to heaven and is calling for a maximum life to redeem a stolen world?* That is, to bring heaven to earth?

To understand kingdom business, maybe we need to understand the mind of God better. God so loved the world that he sent his only Son so that the world could be reconciled to him. Did this love just start at that moment? Why did the world need to be reconciled? I think we could all agree that man was created out of God's love and that the world needed to be reconciled because man was filled with disbelief in the garden. From the moment of the fall of man from relationship with God, his plan was for the redemption of man. If we look at the gospel record, we will find several examples of Jesus talking about this very thing. At least from Abraham to the present day, God has had little else in mind but to open the way for the world to be reconciled to him. *The weak link in this plan has always been the people he chose and their propensity to walk in their self-centered fallen nature—the very thing that God desires to deliver us from.* It is an interesting thing, this deliverance of God from self. It is a gift of God to us, but it can be received by us only when we put us aside and live our lives delivering this gift to others. That is what kingdom business is all about: letting God serve this kingdom to us, so we can serve it to others.

This is step one in the entrance into this kingdom of God: death to self, alive to God. Much is said about being born again, but little is said about death to self. **"I tell you the truth, unless a kernel of wheat falls to the ground and dies, it remains only a single seed. But if it dies, it produces many seeds" (John 12:24).** This "death to self—alive to God" is very important to understand. We must die before we can be reborn. You cannot serve two masters; you cannot be two people. You will serve the one and hate the other. You will end up like the wretched man of Romans 7, trying to serve one but always ultimately serving the other. Or, perhaps you will be like the person of James 1, full of doubt, driven like a wave on the sea, double minded and unstable in all you do. Why is it that this seems to be the fate of so many Christians? No matter how hard we try, the result just seems to be mediocre. Yet there are others who seem to try very little and yet have the formula for a spectacular life in God. The answer lies in very simple expectations.

The first group expects that they must to do something to earn the new man, and the second group knows it is a gift from God and that all they must do is believe. The first group becomes frustrated trying to overcome the sin of the old man. The second group believes the old man is dead and that God has created the new man and consequently pays little attention to the dead old man. They trust that what the Holy Spirit has begun, he will finish. It is very hard to believe, but it is all up to God. **Ephesians 2:8–9** says, **"For it is by grace you have been saved, through faith—and this not from yourselves, it is the gift of God—not by works, so that no one can boast."**

Romans 9:12 says, "not by works but by him who calls."

The scriptural evidence for this reborn experience, this "new man," is overwhelming.

"In reply Jesus declared, 'I tell you the truth, no one can see the kingdom of God unless he is born again'" (John 3:3).

"For you have been born again, not of perishable seed, but of imperishable, through the living and enduring word of God" (1 Peter 1:23).

"For we know that our old self was crucified with him so that the body of sin might be done away with, that we should no longer be slaves to sin" (Romans 6:6).

"You were taught, with regard to your former way of life, to put off your old self, which is being corrupted by its deceitful desires" (Ephesians 4:22).

"... and to put on the new self, created to be like God in true righteousness and holiness" (Ephesians 4:24).

... and have put on the new self, which is being renewed in knowledge in the image of its Creator" (Colossians 3:10).

But I am concerned that maybe we are no longer on the same page. When I use phrases such as *old self* or *born again,* I'm assuming they mean the same thing to both of us. Okay, we all know what assuming does to you and me. Therefore, I will as simply as possible explain why we need to be born again, how to be born again, and the "what now?" when we are born again.

CHAPTER 3

Why

I have previously said there is much to learn from the garden and the experience of Adam and Eve. When we speak of a born-again experience, returning to the beginning is the place to begin. Most of the time, talk of the salvation rebirth begins with us and our need to change. That is just the wrong place by several thousand years.

In the beginning, God created Adam and Eve in his image and breathed into them his Spirit. He then put them into a perfect environment. He instructed them not to eat of the Tree of Knowledge of Good and Evil, for in that day they would die. **"[B]ut you must not eat from the tree of the knowledge of good and evil, for when you eat of it you will surely die" (Genesis 2:17).**

That is the why of why we need to be reborn. On the day Adam ate of the apple, something died within all men for all time.

God promised in that day they would die. I have been told that it is not that they actually died that day, but that death entered the world that day. If that were true, and physical death was not present before the bite, why was there a need for the Tree of Life, and why did God need to remove Adam and Eve from the garden of Eden so that they would not eat from the Tree of Life and live forever?

God said they would die that day, and I don't believe he stuttered. Something in them died that day, as evidenced by the radical change in Adam and Eve. Before, they communed with God, and now, they hid from him. It is very important to understand that God did not change toward them.

Have you ever had a friend with whom you shared a passion and the exercise of that passion had a language of its own? It may be as simple as cross-stitch or as complicated as NASCAR racing, but you could talk for hours using the language of the discipline. (I neither know how to cross-stitch or understand NASCAR racing.) Then maybe your passion changes, and maybe you become a horse enthusiast, specializing in Western Pleasure, a whole new language, one that your friend simply cannot understand. The friendship suffers and perhaps even dies.

As with all analogies, this is not perfect, but it does somewhat sum up what happened when Adam and Eve ate of the Tree of Knowledge Good and Evil. First of all, the problem is not that they were disobedient, as some would contend. No, rather it is what happened in their disobedience. They changed! Something died!

They had regular and personal communication with the triune God. Satan came along and began to dispute what God had said. First, he cast doubt on what God said. **"Now the serpent was more crafty than any of the wild animals the Lord God had made. He said to the woman, 'Did God really say, "You must not eat *from any tree* in the garden"?'" (Genesis 3:1, italics mine).** He knew the truth but chose a lie. He knew that God restricted them from only one tree and that that was for their own good. When I read that Scripture, I can almost hear the sarcasm in his voice, as if he is saying, "He said what? What is wrong with him? He must be hiding something from you."

Eve plays right along, even putting words into God's mouth. **"""...
and you must not touch it, or you will die"""** (Genesis 3:3).
I do not recall God saying anything about touch.

Now that Satan has Eve talking and doubting, the victory is easily
won.

First he openly disputes God: **"'You will not surely die,' the
serpent said to the woman" (Genesis 3:4).** Then he quickly
follows with a false promise: **"'For God knows that when you
eat of it your eyes will be opened, and you will be like God,
knowing good and evil'" (Genesis 3:5).** I find it very interesting
that the Devil used the same motivation on Eve that caused him to fall
from his exalted place—namely, to be like God. Even more interesting,
Adam and Eve were already like God. They were made in his image.

I do not want to go far afield here, but any time we doubt the Word,
we are in a conversation with the Devil, and he will win. If we
begin to question what it means, the Devil will twist the Word to
water it down. We are much better off trying to overbelieve than to
underbelieve.

In Genesis 3:5 the Devil told Eve exactly what would happen: their
eyes would be opened, and like God, they would know good from
evil. What the Devil did was use a truth to create a lie. Adam and
Eve understood the Devil to say that when they ate of the apple,
they would have all the attributes of God, as if God was withholding
something from them. Actually, God was protecting them from the
knowledge of evil. They already had the knowledge of good, for
they knew God, and he is good. It was evil that they were coming
face-to-face with and learning to obey.

The Devil said, "You will be like God, knowing good and evil," as
if the entire essence and character of God is made up of knowing

good from evil. They already had the entire essence and character of God, plus open communication with him. The only thing withheld from them was this knowledge of evil. When they received this knowledge, innocence died. Now they had the ability to judge, the ability to condemn, and the ability to see ugliness. Before, they sought the presence of God; now they considered themselves unworthy and hid from him.

Do not misunderstand: there is a difference between knowing right from wrong and knowing of good and evil. The first deals with our actions, the second with our character. Judging someone's actions does not necessarily tell you about his character.

For every action, there is an equal and opposite reaction! God said, "In that day you will die," and they did. But equally important to our ultimate destiny is the fact that in that day, something was born. Religion is the need for man to contemplate his unworthiness and try to do something to earn God's love. Adam and Eve saw their nakedness and tried to cover it with a fig leaf. They were not hiding from God because they had been disobedient. They were hiding from God because their eyes were opened and they could see not only their nakedness but also the glorified clothing of God. Before the apple incident, they were naked before God and he accepted them, and even more important, they accepted themselves. Nothing changed with God after the bite; he still came looking for them. The only change was with Adam and Eve. What changed? What died?

It is hard to express the true essence of what died. It is much easier to see the results of the death. And they are legion. That is to say, the changes that took place in that moment of time are probably enough to fill a book. However, I'm just going to hit the high points and those that are pertinent to this book.

23

1) Spirituality (innocence) died and religion (judgment) was born. Before the fall, **they were naked and had no shame (Genesis 2:25).** After the fall, they hid from God because they judged themselves as not being good enough. They tried to make themselves acceptable to God by covering themselves with fig leaves.

2) Access to eternal life died; death and decay were born. **"And God commanded the man, saying of every tree of the garden you may freely eat" (Genesis 2:16).** The single exception was the Tree of Knowledge of Good and Evil. Included in the list of every tree was the Tree of Life. However, as we look at the next chapter, after the apple incident, we find that God removed their access not only to the Tree of Life but to all the trees of the garden. **"God said, behold the men has become as one of us, to know good and evil and now lest he put forth his hand and take also of the tree of life and eat and live forever—therefore God sent him forth from the garden of Eden" (Genesis 3:22–23).**

3) A life of ease and blessing to a life of toil and curses. **"Then the Lord God took the man and put him in the Garden of Eden to tend and keep it" (Genesis 2:15 NKJV).** Originally, God created man to tend and keep the perfect garden that he created for him. This is further proved by the Scripture. **"There remains, then, a Sabbath rest for the people of God; for anyone who enters God's rest also rests from his own work, just as God did from his" (Hebrews 4:9–10).** Basically, as we trust God, he simplifies our lives and asks us to simply tend and keep our garden. Contrast this to what happened to man after the fall: **"'Cursed is the ground because of you; through painful toil you will eat of it all the days of your life. It will produce thorns and thistles for you, and you will**

**eat the plants of the field. By the sweat of your brow
you will eat your food'" (Genesis 3:17–19).**

This is just a thumbnail sketch of what happened. The repercussions
are nearly endless, and women fared much worse than men. The bite
of the apple was the beginning of menstrual cramps, childbirth pains,
and being subservient to men. **"to the woman he said, 'I will greatly
increase your pains in childbearing; with pain you will give
birth to children; and your desire shall be for your husband,
and he shall rule over you'" (Genesis 3:16).**

There are places in the New Testament where Paul says he isn't sure
but this is what he believes. Well, I'm not sure what died, but this
is what I believe. We are made in the image of God. He is a triune
God, Father, Son, and Holy Ghost; therefore I believe we are created
a triune being, body, soul, and spirit.

Eve followed the creature and Adam followed Eve, and they used
their souls (emotion and reason) to choose their way instead of
following the Creator and using their spirits (trust and obedience).
As a result, their spirits died and they committed men for all time to
choose their way using emotion and reason.

The reborn man makes decisions by the Spirit.

**[I]n the same way no one knows the thoughts
of God except the Spirit of God we do not
receive the spirit of the world but the Spirit
who is from God that we may understand what
God has freely given us. This is what we speak,
not in words taught us by human wisdom
but in words taught by the Spirit, expressing
spiritual truths in spiritual works. The man
without the spirit does not accept the things**

that come from the Spirit of God, for they are foolishness to him, and he cannot understand them, because they are spiritually discerned. (1 Corinthians 2:11–14)

The answer to the question of why we need to be born again is quite simple. If we have not been born again, we are spiritually dead. Since Adam and Eve made the choice to use the way of this world—that is, the Devil's way to use reason and emotion to make their decisions— they died and committed every member of the Adamic race since then to be born spiritually dead.

When Adam and Eve chose to believe the Devil instead of God, they chose the way of the world and literally became followers of Satan. As we are born of the seed of Adam and Eve, we also were born as followers of the way of the world, and we know who the ruler of the world is. **"As for you, you were dead in your transgressions and sins, in which you used to live when you followed the ways of this world and of the ruler of the kingdom of the air, the spirit who is now at work in those who are disobedient (Ephesians 2:1–2).**

It does not matter if we have been members of the church for forty years, whether we have been on the church council, whether our fathers were members before us, whether we are good people, whether we live by the Golden Rule, whether we pray, or any of the multitude of reasons we can give why we are going to heaven when we die: unless we are born again, we are not. If good deeds could get us there, then many Muslims, Jews, Hindus, and any other devout people would get there before us.

On Martin Luther King Day 2011 the governor of Tennessee in a speech declared that unless you are born again, you're not his brother or sister. He, of course, was greatly ostracized in the news, by the liberal left and even many so-called Christian churches. Equally unsurprising, he backpedaled.

Although his remarks were probably not sensitive or politically correct, they were absolutely on-the-mark spiritually correct.

There are but two families on earth, the one of this world and the one of the kingdom. You are born into the world family, and you can be reborn into the kingdom family. The first you had no choice; the second you choose after you are called. But to be a member of the second, you must give up membership in the first, something we will discuss in more detail later.

In a nutshell, the why of why you need to be born again is that until you are born again, you are dead to the things of God.

Now, it seemed to take a long time to get here, but as I said earlier, there is probably no part of this good news of Jesus Christ that has been more understated and misstated than this salvation message. We have wanted to make it about heaven or hell, sin or holiness, or a whole bunch of other choices. It is not. It is about citizenship.

We must make a choice between citizenship in this evil kingdom of the world or citizenship in the kingdom of God. It is that simple.

That is why, and I'll now tell you how and then the "what now?"

CHAPTER 4

How

I am fairly certain that this will be the shortest chapter. I contend that God does everything simply, and the simplest thing of all is getting on the right side of him.

Before we begin, I would like you to go to the kitchen and get a nice cup of tea, or coffee, or juice, or whatever it is you want. On the way to the kitchen I would like you to consider four questions:

1) Do you believe God is calling you to a deeper walk with him?
2) Do you want a deeper walk with God?
3) Do you believe the words of Jesus found in John 14:6, "I am the way and the truth and the life. No one comes to the Father except through me"?
4) Are you willing to give up the life you presently have and enter into Jesus Christ and the kingdom of God?

Okay, you are back. You have your beverage and are comfortable. Here we go.

If you answered yes to the above questions, you are already there. God reads the intentions of our hearts and the thoughts of our minds and is not nearly as concerned with the words of our mouths as he is with the previous two. However, **Romans 10:10** says, "**For it is with your heart that you believe and are justified, and it is with your mouth that you confess and are saved.**" So, to solidify in our mind what just happened, let's take the four questions above, change them a little bit, and repeat them to ourselves and our Father in heaven.

1) Father, I believe you're calling me to a deeper walk with you. Thank you.
2) Father, I want a deeper walk with you.
3) Father, I believe in your son Jesus Christ as the only way I can ever come to you, for I know I have nothing to give you, and he has bought it all for me with his sacrifice and love.
4) Father, I give up my present carnal life in this world, and I'm asking you to teach me the ways of your kingdom that I may duplicate your Son as he lived on this earth.

There, that's finished. Now let's get on to some work.

Oh, wait a minute, you say, *I don't need that, for I have been saved for X number of years. Obviously, you're talking just to those who have never been saved or have never been Christians.*

No, that is not the case. Most likely when you got saved, you very successfully answered through number three, but have we ever really considered number four? That is what this book is all about.

Let us take a moment and consider number four. The key to number four is not what we're getting but what we're giving up. That is our *present carnal life in this world.* What all exactly does that mean? It is so all encompassing to our present life that it would take volumes to explain it all and explain it exactly. It actually may be impossible. However, as a start, we can say it will mean giving up using our intellect and emotions to make decisions. We can also say it means giving up what the world thinks, and for that matter, what we think the world thinks of us. It means considering that all of our promotions in the world are actually orchestrated by the Father for the kingdom's benefit and not because of any self-possessed abilities and are of no importance except as it pertains to the furtherance of the kingdom of God and our pleasure and enjoyment (which is very important to God).

It means giving up the law, and it means giving up the thought that God has anything in mind for us but good things. It means giving up violence and vengeance. It means giving up the past and letting go, so God can heal us into the future. It also means freely accepting the good things that God has for us, knowing that we deserve them because of Jesus Christ and our relationship with him. And most of all and maybe hardest of all, it means giving up judgment of ourselves and of others.

In summation, it means letting God be an Abba Father to us. That is one whose love we can depend on and who can depend upon us to love him and people without conditions. It means we understand that all of the attributes that God calls us to, such as kindness, goodness, and gentleness, are his attributes. He tells us to forgive all who may have wronged us, because he desires that we would be like him, and he forgives all. He tells us to bless those who curse us, because he is a blesser.

This is the God of the kingdom; this is the one we must know if we are to prosper in the kingdom. To know this God of love and mercy, we must let go of a lot of paradigms in Christianity. The "what now?" of the next chapter is about letting go of these paradigms to see the kingdom of God in a new way.

CHAPTER 5

The "What Now?"

The why may have been the longest chapter and the how may have been the shortest chapter, but the "what now?" is the hardest chapter to write. The reason this is the hardest chapter to write is not that our journeys in the Lord henceforth are going to be so different from each other. In truth they will not be; they will parallel and intersect and all travel down the same road. We are all part of each other, and are all one in Christ, his body. And although he works with us as individual parts of the one body, this working with us follows basically the same pattern for all. He blesses us, protects us, heals us, and brings us to a higher place, and then expects us to do the same for all those around us.

No, it's not where we are going that makes it hard, but rather where we have been. Each of our journeys to get us to this point has been different. The needs, habits, thoughts, and all that goes into making us who we are when we accept Jesus Christ needs to change.

"Therefore, if anyone is in Christ, he is a new creation; the old has gone, the new has come!" (2 Corinthians 5:17).

"Or don't you know that all of us who were baptized into Christ Jesus were baptized into his death? We were therefore buried with him through baptism into death in order that,

just as Christ was raised from the dead through the glory of the Father, *we too may live a new life*" (Romans 6:4, italics mine).

"For we know that our old self was crucified with him" (Romans 6:6).

The above Scriptures seem to indicate that as soon as we receive Christ, we are new creatures, and this is so, except like everything from God, we must believe it to receive it. Perhaps God sees us as new creatures, but the world sees us as much the same old creatures who existed before we received Christ. Truly, there may have been some change, but the flesh—that is, our worldly habits, thought patterns, fears, and all that define who we are—remain largely the same.

We may wrap the flesh in a new cloak such as church work or new ways of speaking, or change our exterior habits and many other things, but the basic me remains unredeemed. I still get angry, I still lack ambition, I still blame others for my problems, and on and on and on.

The pastor who has an affair with the church secretary had a problem with lust before he was saved. The overbearing lady who runs the Sunday school program had a problem with control before she was saved. The TV evangelist who sells trinkets promising much had a problem with greed before he was saved. The Christian employee who cannot get along with other employees had anger issues before he was saved; now he can just blame his fellow employees because they are heathens and not Christians.

This saved-but-unredeemed condition of the church is why it has as many or more divorces than the world, why there is as much unfaithfulness in marriage, and why people cannot stay in one church or get along with others in Christianity. This condition is why

Christianity gets a bad rap. People look at it as powerless to change lives. This hypocrisy need not be, for God's desire is to heal the inner man so we can present his Son to the world.

We assume that as long as we live a minimal Christian life—or on the other hand, if we work hard in the church—everything is okay. Neither condition is God's will for us. He does not need our lip service or any other service, for that matter, unless it is done by a healed soul so that it can be done in a way that glorifies the Father.

Many years ago, I worked for a large retail company and was at a training session at the home office. Managers were there from all over the country, and a moment's topic of conversation was a large renovation another retailer was doing. They were upgrading their product line and refurbishing all of their stores. Some were very concerned that this was going to adversely affect us, but one of the men present said he was not concerned because, in his words, "If you put a suit on a sow, all you have is a well-dressed pig." I knew immediately what he meant. The competing retailer could have the best-looking store and the perfect selection of merchandise, and they still would not compete with us. Why? you ask. They could not compete because their hearts were not right toward the customer. The owner of the company I worked for put a sign in the front of every one of his stores, personally guaranteeing the satisfaction of *his* customers. To the other chain, the customer was a means to an end, but to us, the customer was the purpose.

What in the world does that story have to do with Christianity? Well, I had to tell the whole story to make the "suit on the sow" remark make sense. I believe oftentimes when we become Christians, all we are doing is putting a suit on a sow and maybe we are not even well-dressed pigs. Like the competitive chain above, we may look better on the outside, but the heart is still not right. The whole purpose of Jesus coming was to heal the heart.

> **Woe to you, teachers of the law and Pharisees, you hypocrites! You are like whitewashed tombs, which look beautiful on the outside but on the inside are full of dead men's bones and everything unclean. In the same way, on the outside you appear to people as righteous but on the inside you are full of hypocrisy and wickedness. (Matthew 23:27–28)**

One day, even though I was neither a teacher nor a leader in the church, I found the above Scripture passage hitting dangerously close to home when it used the word *hypocrite*. It hit close enough to me that my heart was stunned, and I began to look within and saw a dead man's bones and an unclean heart.

As I began to seek the Lord about the inside of my cup, he told me that as I released it to him, he would heal me so I could clean the inside of my cup.

The Lord told me something that was impressed upon my heart forever. He said, "Stop trying to be pleasing to me by pleasing me, but rather start being pleasing to me by letting me please you."

I was so worried about presenting the right shine on the outside of my cup that I ignored an awful lot of what was happening on the inside. I had to make a lot of excuses and blame a lot of other people to justify the difference between the inside and the outside.

Like Adam, I would say to the Lord, "It is that woman you gave me," or like Flip Wilson, I might say, "The Devil made me do it," but never would I admit that it was just the old unredeemed man that made me do something.

God was telling me it is his pleasure to heal so that we can taste the finest fruits he has for us. That is the fruits of the kingdom of God.

Once upon a time, my wife and I were having a conversation with another couple, who began talking about a time when they were separated—something my wife and I have also been. It was a very rough time for the man, and just as he began to heal, his wife wanted to get back together.

As he did not want the life that they had had, he told her that because it was the right thing to do, he would get back together, but she was going to be required to do everything he said. In other words, he was going to be head of his family.

The wife said this was a very scary situation for her, but because God had told her, "I will give you another chance, but get it right this time," she knew she had to let her husband be the head.

Both the husband and the wife related how she failed often, but the husband was patient and forgiving, and neither knew quite why it was different this time. He did not understand why the old feelings of distrust, betrayal, and insecurity were no longer there.

As we discussed it, it became obvious that the wife had had a change of heart. Whereas before, she had just given lip service to being a submissive wife and never really had any intention of submitting, now she was really submitting. She often failed, but with humility she would admit her failure and take responsibility for it, something she had never done before.

Because she truly wanted to do right and accepted responsibility for her failures, her husband was able to forgive her, absolve her, and most important of all, trust in her. Eventually, she became better and better at allowing her husband to be the leader, until he praised her for it.

This got me to thinking about God and his relationship with us and, more important, our relationship with him.

Matthew 7:21–23 has always puzzled me. **"Not everyone who says to me, 'Lord, Lord,' will enter the kingdom of heaven, but only he who does the will of my Father who is in heaven. Many will say to me on that day, 'Lord, Lord, did we not prophesy in your name, and in your name drive out demons and perform many miracles?' Then I will tell them plainly, 'I never knew you. Away from me, you evildoers!'"**

On the one hand, most Scriptures talk about unconditional love and forgiveness of sin past, present, and future, and then we have a few Scriptures like this one. They seem to be saying, *Toe the line or you are lost.* Could the answer simply be found in the above story? Could it be that it is not so much what we say or even what we do as it is a condition of the heart and our desire to obey?

The first state of the woman above was that she simply gave lip service to submitting to her husband's will with no real intention of doing so. She had ample excuses for why her way was better, and justification for her actions. It was always somebody else's fault, and she took no responsibility. The second state of the same woman was 180 degrees different from the first. A change of heart turned her around. Before, it was her way or no way, and now it was her desire to fulfill her husband's plan for life. She did not always succeed, but in her failures, she took responsibility and tried again.

The Lord said, "Away from me. I never knew you." If he never knew us, would that mean we never knew him? Is it possible to use the power of the Lord for our own purposes, wills, and self-glory? Could those people whom he never knew be ones who never really knew him with their hearts?

I suppose all the people in this passage would say they know God. Most would say they know Jesus, but God says he never knew them. I don't think it's as important that we can say we know God as it is that we know God knows us. I think this knowing of us must have a lot to do with our doing the will of God.

Like the woman who claimed to be submissive to her husband and yet manipulated her own will are the Christians who say they know God and yet do not carry out his will.

In the body of Christ great emphasis is put upon getting saved but little about carrying out God's will. When we do talk about this will of God, it always seems like a hard thing—witnessing to everyone we know, going to Africa, working hard in our local churches, praying and fasting, and so on. It gets kind of depressing if you think about it, and even worse if you try to do it.

I once heard the will of God described like this: it is not the "determined resolve of God" but rather the "gracious design" for our lives. The keyword in Matthew 7:21 is *heaven*. Do the will of my Father who is in *heaven*. What is this will God has for me in heaven but to live life and live it abundantly and pour out this abundant life into others?

John 10:9–10 says, "'I am the gate; whoever enters through me will be saved. He will come in and go out, and find pasture. The thief comes only to steal and kill and destroy; I have come that they may have life, and have it to the full.'"

The will of the Father was to send the Son, that we may have life and have it in abundance. Not life somewhere in the future, and not just life, but full life now. Jesus describes himself as the gate through which we are saved. That is, he is the access to this abundant life, and he said through that, we will be saved. The word *saved* is an encompassing word, meaning "all of me rescued, delivered, and overcoming everything."

If this rescued, delivered, and overcoming everything life is supposed to be ours, then why not? If God wants it and it sounds good to me, why don't I have it? The answer to that question can be multiple answers or even one single thing that keeps us from receiving God's very best. Within each of us are multiple blockages to receiving all he has for us.

It can be our intellect saying *It does not make sense,* or *If it's true, why haven't I been taught that before?* It can be our emotions saying, *I don't deserve this; I'm just a miserable poor sinner.* It can be our past, our present, or even a fear of the future.

It can be that we were physically, emotionally, or even sexually abused sometime in the past. This type of abuse often shuts down our receptors to receive and makes it hard for us to not be in control.

John 10:10 says that the thief [that is, the Devil] comes to rob, steal and kill.

He is the ruler of the world, and everyone has been damaged by the world. It is his business to damage us. It does not matter if you are eight months or eighty years old; there is damage, and God is in the business of healing that damage so that you can enjoy abundant life.

Say an eight-month-old, perfectly healthy baby is put to bed and decides to test the waters by crying and pitching a fit. Knowing that the child is perfectly fine, the parent lets him work his way through it. The Devil will bring emotions of loneliness and abandonment to that child, and damage is done. On the other hand, if the parent rushes in and comforts the child every time he cries, damage is done.

This being damaged by the world is inevitable. It is the meaning of washing feet. Jesus said, "A person who has had a bath needs only to wash his feet; his whole body is clean." We have had a bath and have been washed clean by the blood of the Lamb; however, our trespass in this world leaves us with dirty feet. That is why James admonishes us to keep ourselves from being polluted by the world.

The above story of the baby almost sounds hopeless: no matter what we do, it is wrong. **"I have told you these things, so that in me you may have peace. In this world you will have trouble. But take heart! I have overcome the world" (John 16:33).** Maybe the story of the baby makes the Scripture come to life. For you see, the baby is put to bed and thinks all is lost because nobody will respond to his demands, but the next morning dawns brightly, and he is met with a smiling face, soft words, a change of diaper, and a belly full of warm food. The distress of the night before is forgotten, and all seems right. Such is the same with us as we have our feet washed clean from the pollution of the world.

"Jesus the greatest" gave us the example of washing the feet and expects us to be healed enough to be feet washers.

This immediate damage the world is trying to impose upon us cannot really damage us if we are of a spirit attitude. If we return evil for evil, we are damaged. If we return good for evil, we are overcoming the evil both in ourselves and in the world.

That is what Paul means in **Romans 12:2**, where he says, **"Do not conform any longer to the pattern of this world, but be transformed by the renewing of your mind. Then you will**

be able to test and approve what God's will is—his good, pleasing and perfect will."

It is only when we break free from the pattern of this world and have our minds renewed that we can find a good, pleasing, and perfect will of God. You will notice that this will of God is described as good, pleasing, and perfect. The Scripture actually means it is good, pleasing, and perfect for and to us from God. But we can find this only as we have been healed from the damage of the world. God is all about healing us so that we can taste the good fruits of him.

However, this struggle to keep ourselves unspotted from the present world is really the easy part. It is the damage that has built up over years or that happened in a moment and shaped our lives from that moment on that are the real tough issues.

This baggage from the past can have many forms, and works itself out in our lives in habitually destructive ways. It can be generational sins, demonic strongholds, learned behavior, or imposed strongholds (abuse of any kind), to name a few. But the worst of all and maybe the hardest to break through is religious strongholds. By religious strongholds I am not just speaking of deliverance from being a Muslim, Buddhist, Hindu, or any other non-Christ-centered religion. I am speaking of traditional Christianity also. Traditional Christianity with its "condemn or condone" and "sinner or saint" cycles is just as destructive.

More often than not in man's judgment we fall into the condemned sinner category rather than condoned saint. Let me make it very clear: we are saints because of what Jesus Christ has done. And once that sainthood is received, we do not become sinners by what we do. Once we fall into the sin/saint cycle, it cuts off our ability to believe God can or will bless someone habitually as evil as ourselves. Now we have denied God the very thing he above all wishes to do.

This healing and deliverance from the baggage of the past is really a twofold process. On the one hand, we need to be healed inside from the hurt that has sunk into our soul. Often we do not even know it is there. An example would be that if we felt deeply, repeatedly rejected as a young child, we might spend our adult lives pushing people away and not even knowing why. This will require an inner healing of that area in our souls that fears and feels rejection. On the other hand, we have formed the habit of pushing people away often by our caustic self-centered actions. Those actions will have to be recognized as sin and repented of. Often apologies have to be given and we repeat this process until trust and love replaces fear of rejection. Often the inner healing is the easy part. The habits we form are safety mechanisms designed to protect and/or gratify self and often are much harder to release. But God is the God of the release, and it is his desire for us to be whole and healthy people.

This is exactly what it is all about, this lifelong healing process that truly makes us people of God, and it is fully and completely the "what now?" Nothing else matters to God as much as this victory over the world and self, for without it, we are not that much good to the kingdom or to ourselves.

This healing process of God is a lifelong process, and no matter how much or how little I have been healed, I need more. And so do you!

"I have come that they [you] may have life, and have it to the full" (John 10:10) becomes alive and real as we cooperate with God in this healing process. So let us begin the work. Whether we have been saved for ten minutes or ten years, now is the time to begin.

John Kennedy said, "Ask not what your country can do for you but what you can do for your country." I believe the Christian ought to ask the opposite: ask not what you can do for your God but rather what God can do for you. And what he can do for you on the inside if you open your heart to him will amaze you and give you eagle's wings.

So walk into his will by opening your heart and asking him to start healing.

All things work for the best for those who love the Lord and are called according to his purpose. And this purpose is that we should live full, emotionally healthy, and prosperous lives in communion with other saints to form the body of Christ.

CHAPTER 6

A Holy Spirit

In the first part of this book I spoke of five principles of God that when believed become life-changing experiences. The five are an exchanged life, a holy spirit, a healed body, a prosperous soul, and a godly character. We have just discussed the first, an exchanged life.

Literally, Jesus Christ exchanged his life for yours. And you have exchanged your life in the world for a new life in the kingdom of God—a death and a birth.

The first principle was all about that death. The second principle is all about the birth. As we explained previously, before we were born again, we were dead to the things of God. I believe what was dead—that is, what died in Adam—was our spirit. What comes alive when we are born again is that spirit connection to God. That is the thing that allows us to agree with Paul when he exclaims, **"We have the mind of Christ" (1 Corinthians 2:16).**

I said that the fourth chapter was going to be the shortest in this book. Well, this could probably be the second shortest. Not because the Holy Spirit does not deserve great consideration but because it is such a contentious subject, I am simply going to tell you my experiences, my beliefs, and the experiences of people I know. You can at that point decide for yourself what you believe and how much you want of the Holy Spirit. My only hope is that you do not deny my experiences.

I thank my Father in heaven for his love poured into my heart, and I thank Jesus Christ, his Son, whose great sacrifice made everything possible for me. But equally, I am eternally grateful to the third person of the Trinity. That is the Holy Spirit of God. It is he who delivers everything heavenly to us: healing for my body, holiness for my mind, and prosperity for my life and my soul. He delivers to me all the gifts and tools I need to lead a successful Christian life. Plus, to the extent I allow him, he gives to me the character of God.

This Holy Spirit of God brings to us everything that is good and gracious and lovely and of good report. Yet there is probably more contention in the body of Christ over the how, when, and where of the Holy Spirit than any other single issue. How do we get this sweet, gentle Spirit, and when and where does he work? All those questions split us right down the middle—or more truthfully, fracture us to pieces. That is precisely why this may be a short chapter. I no longer want to take part in the endless dialogue about the sweet nature of God referred to as the Holy Spirit. As I said before, I'm simply going to tell you my experiences and what I believe, and you can make up your own mind.

In 1 Corinthians 12:7–10 is a list of nine gifts for us from the Holy Spirit. In Galatians 5:22–23 is a list of nine fruits for us from the Holy Spirit. There is a story that I heard many years ago about the Jewish high priest entering into the Holy of Holies once a year to offer sacrifice for the sins of the people. According to legend, he had a rope tied to his ankle. On the hem of his garment were nine bells. The purpose of the bells was so that those outside the temple could hear them and know that the sacrifices were being made. However, if the bells stopped ringing, they would know that the high priest had entered the Holy of Holies unworthily and had died. The purpose of the rope was so that they could pull him out without anybody else entering the inner sanctuary of God. Each of these bells was tuned to a particular note, and with the normal movement of the robes, the combination would make a very harmonious result. The problem was that if the bells hit one another, the tones were lost and a noise resulted. Therefore, a tassel was placed between each bell that prevented them from touching one another, nine tassels to harmonize the nine bells. According to New Testament legend, the bells represented the gifts of the Spirit and the tassels represented the fruits of the Spirit.

I do not know if this legend is actually true. It has, however, always presented a great word picture for me. If both the gifts and the fruits of the Holy Spirit were functioning together in his people, we would see the kingdom of God among us. If we have too much gift and not enough fruit, we are just noisy bells. On the other hand, if we are all fruit and no gift, we might be dead and not even know it.

The Holy Spirit has basically two jobs in this world: to protect us from the world, the flesh, and the Evil One; and to show the world the true character of God. Imagine the short time it would take to evangelize the world if every Christian always exhibited the nine fruits of the spirit. If we were always filled with **love, joy, peace, patience, goodness, kindness, gentleness, faithfulness, and self-control (Galatians 5:22)**, one of two things would happen: either people would see the character of God in his people and beg to have the same or they would turn against it and be lost.

Either way "the die would be cast" and the kingdom would come. Why? Because if we truly exhibited the Spirit of Christ, the evil world would simply cease to be. The nine fruits of the Spirit are the character of Christ, for the Holy Spirit is the Spirit of the Father and the Son.

Let us imagine further that we all belonged to a church in which someone had at least one of the nine gifts of the Spirit (1 Corinthians 12:8). Think of the comfort we would have, knowing we were part of a body that could heal itself of any disease, because people in that body had gifts that could heal all manner of disease and sickness. Or if we knew someone had a gift of miracles that could produce something out of nothing, or a gift of discerning spirits so we could see what the Devil was up to. How about if we knew there were ones who could read God's mind (word of wisdom) and tell us how to proceed with that will (word of knowledge)? Would we not be fearless?

I really like the way the Word expresses our relationship with the gifts. **The gifts are distributed individually for the benefit of all (1 Corinthians 12:7).** It's a body thing.

Imagine what it would be like if we all always functioned in the fruits and exercised the gifts. Wait—why should we just have to imagine? These are the fruits of the Spirit and the gifts of the Spirit, and if we were filled with the Spirit, why would we not have them? Doesn't it make sense that if we truly were filled, the character and purpose of that which filled us would be evident always? Why not? Why do we not see more of the fruits and the gifts every day, always?

If we listen to the Word, the obvious answer has to be that we are not putting to death the deeds of the flesh, for it is only then that the Spirit can fulfill his destiny in our lives.

It would seem that Paul pretty well describes how most of us feel in **Romans 7:18 "I know that nothing good lives in me, that is, in my sinful nature. For I have the desire to do what is good, but I cannot carry it out."**

Why does the sinful nature seem so predominant in our lives? Why is the cry of our heart often the echo of the man of **Romans 7:19,** which says **"For what I do is not the good I want to do; no, the evil I do not want to do—this I keep on doing."**

Paul gives us the answer very simply in **Galatians 5:16–17**, where he says, **"So I say, live by the Spirit, and you will not gratify the desires of the sinful nature. For the sinful nature desires what is contrary to the Spirit and the Spirit what is contrary to the sinful nature. They are in conflict with each other, so that you do not do what you want."**

You will notice it does not say stop sinning and you will be full of the Spirit; rather it says live by the Spirit and you will not fulfill the flesh. We are much too preoccupied with sin. Sin does not keep us from being full of the Holy Spirit. Rather, not being full of the Holy Spirit allows us to go on sinning.

Then how does this filling up happen? Well, I believe from my experience and from the experiences of those whose filling I respect that it is a double experience with continuing maintenance.

Allow me to explain from my own experience. Forty years ago, I was a member of large denomination but never was told of the saving grace of Jesus Christ. However, my heart was hungry. My job at that time had me traveling throughout the Midwest, and everywhere I went, I heard rumors of something happening. It was something new, yet something old, and mostly something just wonderful. It was all very mysterious and somewhat hidden. People talked of an underground church, a church within a church, and the more I heard, the more I wanted to hear.

Yet in my own hometown I heard nothing. I even asked a few questions, and no one seemed to know much. But God let someone know of my hunger, for out of the blue, my wife and I were asked to a daylong seminar. As I recall, we knew no one in the room.

After she heard the first speaking in tongues, my wife wanted to escape from those crazy people, but I was hooked. The more I heard, the more I wanted to hear. Well, the seminar lasted all day, as I remember, but it was not enough, and I asked my wife if I could invite two of the men over to our house after the meeting, which I believe ended about 5:30 p.m. She said no, absolutely not in her house, and I said, "Well, they are coming to my house for a little while." I believe they left around 4:30 a.m., but those hours changed my life forever.

They talked for hours, and I asked endless questions. They patiently answered each one, and each answer brought a new battery of questions. Although they were great at answering my questions, they were not very good at closing. Finally, after several hours—and not because I had run out of questions but because I was so hungry for what they had—I almost screamed the question, "What must I do to be saved?"

I was so abrupt that my two mentors were momentarily taken aback, but they quickly recovered and led me through the magic words. And it worked. For the first time in my life, I felt accepted, but more important, I felt worthy of acceptance. Suddenly, I belonged. In that brief second, my personal order moved from chaos to cosmos. My universe had moved from the earthly to the heavenly, and I was content.

But neither God nor man would allow me to be in that state. With a single question my mentors changed my contentedness to something else. As I responded to the question, I became more spiritually hungry than I ever imagined possible. They asked the question straightforwardly and without hesitation, and my response was just as sudden and frank.

The question was "Now that you are saved, would you like to receive the Holy Spirit?" I was blissfully ignorant and had no "doubt causing Holy Spirit theology," so my response was "Why wouldn't I?" Apparently my mentors could think of no reason why I shouldn't, because they immediately laid hands on me. In that fraction of a second between their hands touching me and before they began to pray, I felt something happening. It was very different from the experience of a few minutes earlier.

The previous experience was one of taking away. When I accepted Jesus Christ, it took away guilt and feelings of extreme unworthiness. It took away feelings of aloneness and despair. And of course there was that adding-on of a great peace, but most of the experience was one of emptying and cleansing. However, when I asked the Holy Spirit to fill me, it was all about making me more. I felt filled with a holy presence and with power, and I immediately began to speak in a language I did not know (tongues). I might describe the first experience as wonderfully quiet but the second as exquisitely loud (but not in a noisy way). There is no doubt in my mind that I had two separate experiences. Both were wonderful, but very different from each other.

My double experience was more than forty years ago and yet is still a vivid and wonderful memory. But I'm not arrogant enough to believe it's the only way. For instance, my wife's experience of salvation and the infilling of the Holy Spirit was much different from mine.

My wife noticed a change in me (it was the only time in nearly fifty years together that I was not telling her what she needed in her life), and as some weeks passed and I maintained my quiet peace, she became envious of it. One day while she was vacuuming, an almost audible voice asked her if she wanted what I had, and she said yes. The voice then instructed her to get on her knees and ask him (Jesus) into her heart and he would be her Lord and Savior. She did and he was.

Norma knew something had changed. It just felt good. However, she did not at this time speak in "another language." As our fellowship continued with other Christians with like beliefs, it was not long before Norma desired to speak in tongues and asked for prayer. When hands were laid upon her, she was filled with the Holy Spirit and began to speak in other tongues as the Spirit enabled her (Acts 2:4).

From the moment Norma first heard tongues, she thought it was odd at best and crazy at worst. She had no desire for and was in fact afraid of the manifestation. As she experienced others around her whom she trusted speaking in tongues as naturally as they did English, she began to believe and appreciate, which was soon followed by desire. However, had she been around people who did not believe in and spoke against tongues, she would have probably never believed to receive.

Like fingerprints and DNA, no two people's salvation experience is exactly alike. Although we each may think that everyone should have an experience like ours, God who makes no two snowflakes alike is very capable of giving each of us a unique and personal path to him. The only coincidence in all of these experiences is that if the path truly leads to the Father, it must come through the Son and will be led by the Holy Spirit.

CHAPTER 7

It's Not All Good

With forty years of experience and having been to conferences and meetings of many different kinds and in many different places, we have seen just about everything. I would like for us to have a discussion about the Holy Spirit and what is legitimate experience—what is from the flesh and what is maybe sometimes from the Evil One.

As the title of this chapter implies, I do not believe everything that is done in the name of Jesus, the Holy Spirit, or the Father is truly of God. On the other hand, let's not throw out the baby with the bathwater. I have been in meetings where I have seen what I consider unnecessary actions done in the name of all three members of the Trinity, but as this chapter is concerned with the Holy Spirit, I will direct my comments there.

We have heard about the excesses, and sometimes we have actually gone to those churches to see firsthand for ourselves, but we have never seen anywhere near the abuses that have been reported. That said, on many occasions we have seen demonstrations that we consider to be of the flesh and have absolutely nothing to do with the Holy Spirit or his work. We attribute these demonstrations to two factors: one is that the people doing them need healing and in some cases, deliverance. They are attention junkies and will do anything to be seen and accepted. The second factor is the failure of the congregation, particularly the leadership, to deal with it.

Oftentimes the actions (abuses) are reported as being much worse than they actually are. The leadership then has a tendency to focus on the exaggerated reporting and ignore the abuses. When questioned, leadership will almost always respond that they do not want to do anything to quench the Holy Spirit. However, it is my considered opinion that when you don't deal with those individuals and their extravagant actions, you quench the Holy Spirit. It seems to me that whenever the flesh is not dealt with and is sometimes even glorified, it becomes the predominant force present.

For purposes of this discussion, let's make three categories of actions attributed to the Holy Spirit. One category consists of those things that have absolutely no purpose and draw more attention to the person than to the Holy Spirit. The second category is made up of those actions that are not mentioned in the Bible but are common among many groups and are just fun. The third group contains those genuine manifestations of the Holy Spirit mentioned in Scripture.

Before we go on, let me do a little backtracking. As I discuss these three categories, I do not want to leave the impression that I believe I am covering every manifestation of any one of the three.

Among the things that have absolutely no purpose are animal noises, any number of unusual tics, and anything the doer claims is beyond his control. There are any numbers of outlandish behaviors that can go on in the body of Christ that are not dealt with. Often doers seem compelled, or testify to a compulsion to perform, and often they consider it a sign that the Spirit is present. As I said above, I believe these demonstrations need to be seriously considered as fleshly or demonic. I must admit I have never been in any type of leadership position in a fellowship or church where this kind of behavior was exhibited, so I cannot give advice based on firsthand knowledge about what course of action to take. I have been told by people who have been involved that when confronted, most times, the person or people doing the actions will leave declaring that you are anti-spiritual.

The somewhat common and just fun group includes dancing in the Spirit, slaying in the Spirit, gold dust, and similar experiences. Although these experiences are not specifically mentioned in the Bible (and I am not going to try to biblically justify them as some have), they are common enough throughout the charismatic community that I am comfortable they are from God. For those of you who are not familiar with these experiences, they are not as weird or frightening as one may think. They're just different from what many of us are accustomed to. I will say this: I enjoy them.

Here's the problem: when they become more important than our relationship with the Holy Spirit, they have become our God. But the same could be said for almost anything, including our liturgies, which I consider the number one killer of the Holy Ghost. It is the person of the Trinity called the Holy Spirit that is to be the center of our focus, not his gifts or demonstrations.

Here are a couple of examples of what I mean. Several years ago, a friend of mine was invited to speak at meeting. When he arrived, he noticed that as the people were arriving, they had tennis shoes over their shoulders and were wearing dress shoes. My friend happened to ask one of the members whether they were going to have a basketball game or something after the service. The reply somewhat shocked him. He was told no, that the shoes were for when they danced in the Spirit. To them it was a foregone conclusion that the Holy Spirit was going to move them to dance. There was no room for other plans by God. They equated dancing in the Spirit with God showing up. Spirituality = dancing in the Spirit.

One time I was at a large convention in Miami when suddenly a buzz went through the convention center that in a certain room there was gold dust. Many people rushed to the room. My friend and I eventually made it down there. It seems that a very flamboyant woman had the ability to wave her hand and goldlike glitter would appear. It was neat; however, more attention seemed to be directed at the woman than at the Holy Ghost. She would pick out individuals seemingly at random and announce to the entire room that God had told her to lay hands on them and they would receive the ability to produce the same phenomenon. One of the people was my friend, who was very excited to receive this gift. However, these many years later, I have yet to see him produce any glitter.

Maybe the only way to really illustrate what I'm trying to say is by presenting two more stories. One time I was at a moderately large meeting and we were into great worship when suddenly a young lady with Down Syndrome removed herself from the crowd and, walking to the back of the room, began to beautifully dance in the Spirit, expressing, maybe the only way she could, her love for the Trinity. She had situated herself in such a way that I do not believe many people noticed, but I know God did.

I've been in other meetings where people felt free to express themselves to the Spirit through the Spirit in this manner. Whenever it has blessed me, they have been inconspicuous and courteous.

The second story is a little bit personal and involves gold dust. The first story I told about gold dust was all about show. It was a showy woman doing a showy thing in a very showy way. The second has none of that, and I am not sure I've even shared it with anybody. Several years ago, a friend and I were driving to another city and talking about our love for the Trinity, especially about the wonder of the Holy Spirit. As we continued to talk, I noticed his face began to shine as if somebody had sprinkled it with glitter. Suddenly, a very strong presence of God was in the car with us. It was a very personal and lovely way for God to say, "I love you."

When a manifestation is of the Holy Spirit, it will be simply functional. It won't be a great show, and he will not exalt a person so that person's flesh is fulfilled. That is sin. When we deny flesh, then the Holy Spirit will bring forth simple function.

The third group is easy to list. It comes straight out of Scripture and is referred to as the manifestations of the Holy Spirit:

> **Now to each one the manifestation of the Spirit is given for the common good. To one there is given through the Spirit the message of wisdom, to another the message of knowledge by means of the same Spirit, to another faith by the same Spirit, to another gifts of healing by that one Spirit, to another miraculous powers, to another prophecy, to another distinguishing between spirits, to another speaking in different kinds of tongues, and to still another the interpretation of tongues. (1 Corinthians 12:7–10)**

There are several comments I want to make about this Scripture, but first I will relist them with a simple and often incomplete description of each. Sometimes in commentaries they are listed in a slightly different way from 1 Corinthians 12. They're listed in three groups of three, and that is the way I shall list them. Group one would be gifts of revelation; first among them, and I believe first among all the gifts, is the gift of the word of wisdom. Simply said, this is the gift of knowing the mind and purpose of God revealed about any single given situation. The companion to the gift of the word of wisdom is the gift of the word of knowledge. The word of knowledge is the

Holy Spirit–given ability to know some fact or piece of knowledge that you have no way of knowing with your human intellect. Once you know this knowledge, the gift of the word of wisdom would tell you how to proceed.

The third gift in this group is called the discerning of spirits. This gift gives the bearer the ability to see into the spirit world. Here is a cute story of a man who came home from a conference to tell his wife that he had seen angels on each side of the speaker that day. After the speaker was finished, the man went up to him and said, "You're very blessed." The speaker was a little confused and the man was a little embarrassed to say he had seen angels. When the speaker realized what was going on, he said to the man, "Did you see my angels," and the man said, "Yes, I did." The speaker said there was a man in his congregation who saw them on a regular basis when he was preaching. Anyway, this man went home and told his wife the story. She said, "I so want that gift," and the man said, "Sometimes you see demons also." The woman then exclaimed, "I so do not want that gift."

The second group of three we will call the gifts of power. The first among these three is a gift of faith. Do not confuse the gift of faith with the fruit of the spirit of faith. I am not going to detail the difference, but they are completely different from each other. The gift of faith, simply put, is an unwavering trust in God for personal or corporate protection or provision in a given situation. Daniel in the lion's den and Elijah being fed by the raven are two examples of the gift of faith. A New Testament example of this gift I believe can be seen in Jesus feeding the multitudes.

The second gift in this group is the gift of working miracles. The gift of miracles defined is "the power of God working through an individual to speak a word by which the laws of nature are suspended or changed." For example, we know a man who can speak to severe weather and it will go around his property. Another example of the working of the gift of miracles is when Jesus walked on water.

The third gift is referred to as gifts of healing. It's interesting that this gift is referred to in the plural. I personally believe this is because no one person has the gift to heal all diseases. Different people have the gift for healing different diseases. For instance, I know a man who prays for people's backs, and their backs are healed.

The third group of three we will refer to as the gifts of voice. For the most part these three gifts require us to give voice to the Holy Spirit. The first of these gifts is the gift of prophecy. This is the ability to hear God somewhere inside you and to lend voice to that leading. We must not confuse the gift of prophecy with the office of a prophet. Everyone who is a prophet will prophesy, but not everyone who prophesies is a prophet. We are told in **1 Corinthians 14:3, "But everyone who prophesies speaks to men for their strengthening, encouragement and comfort."** You will notice that there is nothing in this descriptive Scripture about prophecy that speaks of revelation. However, the office of a prophet as listed in the fivefold ministry of Ephesians 4:11 is all about revelation. The prophet reveals to us using primarily the gift of word knowledge and the gift of the word of wisdom, opening to us the mind and purpose of God.

Prophecy is a gift given to the body of Christ to strengthen us, to encourage us, and to comfort us. Usually, this gift is used in a corporate gathering, but it can work when speaking to either an individual or a group.

The next gift I would like to speak about is the gift of interpretation of tongues. This gift is the ability to interpret a message that has been given in a tongue. I do not believe this gift is usually a literal translation, but it is possible.

Lastly, I will speak about the gift of various kinds of tongues. Tongues are usually the first and easiest of the nine gifts to receive. Some people contend it is the sign that one has received the baptism of the Holy Spirit. I will not contend this one way or the other; however, I must say that those whom I perceive as being baptized in the Holy Spirit speak in tongues. Speaking in tongues is simply the God-given ability to speak to him in a language you do not know, thereby short-circuiting the intellect. This speaking may take the form of praise, intercession, or personal requests. The language is given to us by the Holy Spirit so we can pray to the Father in a much more perfect way. Neither our "I wanter" or our intellect gets in the way of our conversation with God. I personally find it a fascinating and wonderful gift.

That is a thumbnail sketch of the nine gifts of the Holy Spirit. Let me stress that by no means did I begin to explain the wonderful fullness of these gifts. In a lifetime of living within the Holy Spirit and functioning in his gifts, you would never exhaust their width or depth.

In case you have any doubts of the magnificent appearance of the Holy Spirit in our lives, the next chapter is simply several pages of Scripture listing what the Holy Spirit does for us, through us, and in us. And it is all good.

CHAPTER 8

The Holy Wow

He teaches us.

"The Holy Spirit will teach you at that time what you should say" (Luke 12:12).

He's our counselor.

"But the Counselor, the Holy Spirit, whom the Father will send in my name, will teach you all things and will remind you of everything I have said to you" (John 14:26).

He is our source of power.

"But you will receive power when the Holy Spirit comes on you; and you will be my witnesses in Jerusalem, and in all Judea and Samaria, and to the ends of the earth" (Acts 1:8).

He enables our prayer language.

"All of them were filled with the Holy Spirit and began to speak in other tongues as the Spirit enabled them" (Acts 2:4).

He is a gift from God.

"Peter replied, 'Repent and be baptized, every one of you, in the name of Jesus Christ for the forgiveness of your sins. And you will receive the gift of the Holy Spirit'" (Acts 2:38).

He emboldens us.

"After they prayed, the place where they were meeting was shaken. And they were all filled with the Holy Spirit and spoke the word of God boldly" (Acts 4:31).

He strengthens us and encourages us.

"Then the church throughout Judea, Galilee and Samaria enjoyed a time of peace. It was strengthened; and encouraged by the Holy Spirit, it grew in numbers, living in the fear of the Lord" (Acts 9:31).

He is our sign of acceptance.

"God, who knows the heart, showed that he accepted them by giving the Holy Spirit to them, just as he did to us" (Acts 15:8).

He puts us in office.

"Keep watch over yourselves and all the flock of which the Holy Spirit has made you overseers. Be shepherds of the church of God, which he brought with his own blood" (Acts 20:28).

He is holiness.

"… and who through the Spirit of holiness was declared with power to be the Son of God by his resurrection from the dead: Jesus Christ our Lord" (Romans 1:4).

Our hearts are circumcised by him.

"No, a man is a Jew if he is one inwardly; and circumcision is circumcision of the heart, by the Spirit, not by the written code. Such a man's praise is not from men, but from God" (Romans 2:29).

He is our love.

"And hope does not disappoint us, because God has poured out his love into our hearts by the Holy Spirit, whom he has given us" (Romans 5:5).

He is the new covenant.

"But now, by dying to what once bound us, we have been released from the law so that we serve in the new way of the Spirit, and not in the old way of the written code" (Romans 7:6).

He is life and peace.

"The mind of sinful man is death, but the mind controlled by the Spirit is life and peace" (Romans 8:6).

He is our belonging.

"You, however, are controlled not by the sinful nature but by the Spirit, if the Spirit of God lives in you. And if anyone does not have the Spirit of Christ, he does not belong to Christ" (Romans 8:9).

He lives in us.

"And if the Spirit of him who raised Jesus from the dead is living in you, he who raised Christ from the dead will also give life to your mortal bodies through his Spirit, who lives in you" (Romans 8:11).

He gives us life.

"[H]e who raised Christ from the dead will also give life to your mortal bodies through his Spirit" (Romans 8:11).

He leads us.

"[T]hose who are led by the Spirit of God are sons of God" (Romans 8:14).

He gives us sonship.

"[Y]ou received the Spirit of sonship" (Romans 8:15).

He tells us we are sons.

"The Spirit himself testifies with our spirit that we are God's children" (Romans 8:16).

He helps our weaknesses.

"In the same way, the Spirit helps us in our weakness. We do not know what we ought to pray for" (Romans 8:26).

He intercedes for us.

"[T]he Spirit himself intercedes for us with groans that words cannot express" (Romans 8:26).

He confirms our conscience in the truth.

"I speak the truth in Christ—I am not lying, my conscience confirms it in the Holy Spirit" (Romans 9:1).

He is our righteousness, peace, and joy.

"For the kingdom of God is not a matter of eating and drinking, but of righteousness, peace and joy in the Holy Spirit, Gal 5:5 But by faith we eagerly await through the Spirit the righteousness for which we hope" (Romans 14:17).

He is our unity.

"May the God who gives endurance and encouragement give you a spirit of unity among yourselves as you follow Christ Jesus" (Romans 15:5).

He is our overflowing hope.

"May the God of hope fill you with all joy and peace as you trust in him, so that you may overflow with hope by the power of the Holy Spirit" (Romans 15:13).

We are sanctified by him.

"… to be a minister of Christ Jesus to the Gentiles with the priestly duty of proclaiming the gospel of God, so that the Gentiles might become an offering acceptable to God, sanctified by the Holy Spirit" (Romans 15:16).

He is our power for signs and miracles.

"… by the power of signs and miracles, through the power of the Spirit. So from Jerusalem all the way around to Illyricum, I have fully proclaimed the gospel of Christ" (Romans 15:19).

He is our revelation of the deep things of God.

"God has revealed it to us by his Spirit. The Spirit searches all things, even the deep things of God" (1 Corinthians 2:10).

Even God's deepest personal thoughts

"For who among men knows the thoughts of a man except the man's spirit within him? In the same way no one knows the thoughts of God except the Spirit of God" (1 Corinthians 2:11).

He gives us understanding of the gifts of God.

"We have not received the spirit of the world but the spirit who is from God, that we may understand what God has freely given us" (1 Corinthians 2:12).

He teaches us to speak God.

"This is what we speak, not in words taught us by human wisdom but in words taught by the spirit, expressing spiritual truths in spiritual words" (1 Corinthians 2:13).

He gives us spiritual discernment.

"The man without the Spirit does not accept the things that come from the Spirit of God, for they are foolishness to him, and he cannot understand them, because they are spiritually discerned" (1 Corinthians 2:14).

He washes us, he sanctifies us, he justifies us.

"And that is what some of you were. But you were washed, you were sanctified, you were justified in the name of the Lord Jesus Christ and by the Spirit of our God" (1 Corinthians 6:11).

He makes us the temple of God.

"Do you not know that your body is a temple of the Holy Spirit, who is in you, whom you have received from God? You are not your own" (1 Corinthians 6:19).

He leads us.

"But if you are led by the Spirit, you are not under law" (Galatians 5:18).

He frees us from sinful nature.

"So I say, live by the Spirit, and you will not gratify the desires of the sinful nature" (Galatians 5:16).

He frees us from legalism.

"[T]hrough Christ Jesus the law of the spirit of life set me free from the law of sin and death" (Romans 8:2).

He reveals the Lordship of Jesus to us.

"Therefore I tell you that no one who is speaking by the Spirit of God says, 'Jesus be cursed,' and no one can say, 'Jesus is Lord,' except by the Holy Spirit" (1 Corinthians 12:3).

He is our seal that God owns us.

"[He] set his seal of ownership on us, and put his Spirit in our hearts as a deposit, guaranteeing what is to come" (2 Corinthians 1:22).

"And you also were included in Christ when you heard the word of truth, the gospel of your salvation. Having believed, you were marked in him with a seal, the promised Holy Spirit" (Ephesians 1:13).

"And do not grieve the Holy Spirit of God, with whom you were sealed for the day of redemption" (Ephesians 4:30).

He is our ministry.

"[W]ill not the ministry of the Spirit be even more glorious?" (2 Corinthians 3:8).

He is our Lord and our freedom.

"Now the Lord is the Spirit, and where the Spirit of the Lord is, there is freedom" (2 Corinthians 3:17).

He transforms us into God's likeness.

"And we, who with unveiled faces all reflect the Lord's glory, are being transformed into his likeness with ever-increasing glory, which comes from the Lord, who is the Spirit" (2 Corinthians 3:18).

He is our fellowship.

"May the grace of the Lord Jesus Christ, and the love of God, and the fellowship of the Holy Spirit be with you all" (2 Corinthians 13:14).

He conflicts our sinful nature.

"For the sinful nature desires what is contrary to the Spirit, and the Spirit what is contrary to the sinful nature. They are in conflict with each other, so that you do not do what you want" (Galatians 5:17).

He is our fruit.

"But the fruit of the Spirit is love, joy, peace, patience, kindness, goodness, faithfulness" (Galatians 5:22).

He is eternal life.

"The one who sows to please his sinful nature, from that nature will reap destruction; the one who sows to please the Spirit, from the Spirit will reap eternal life" (Galatians 6:8).

He is our wisdom and revelation.

"I keep asking that the God of our Lord Jesus Christ, the glorious Father, may give you the Spirit of wisdom and revelation, so that you may know him better" (Ephesians 1:17).

He is our access to the Father.

"For through him we both have access to the Father by one Spirit" (Ephesians 2:18).

He makes us into God's dwelling.

"And in him you too are being built together to become a dwelling in which God lives by his Spirit" (Ephesians 2:22).

He is the revelation of God's plan.

"… which was not made known to men in other generations as it has now been revealed by the Spirit to God's holy apostles and prophets" (Ephesians 3:5).

He is the strength of our inner being.

"I pray that out of his glorious riches he may strengthen you with power through his Spirit in your inner being" (Ephesians 3:16).

He is our primary offensive weapon.

"Take the helmet of salvation and the sword of the Spirit, which is the word of God" (Ephesians 6:17).

He is our most effective way to pray.

"And pray in the Spirit on all occasions with all kinds of prayers and requests. With this in mind, be alert and always keep on praying for all the saints" (Ephesians 6:18).

He is our help.

"For I know that through your prayers and the help given by the Spirit of Jesus Christ, what has happened to me will turn out for my deliverance" (Philippians 1:19).

He is our fellowship.

"If you have any encouragement from being united with Christ if any comfort from his love, if any fellowship with the Spirit if any tenderness and compassion, …" (Philippians 2:1).

He is how we worship.

"For it is we who are the circumcision, we who worship by the Spirit of God, who glory in Christ Jesus, and who put no confidence in the flesh" (Philippians 3:3).

He gives us the messages of God.

"You became imitators of us and of the Lord; in spite of severe suffering, you welcomed the message with the joy given by the Holy Spirit" (1 Thessalonians 1:6).

He sanctifies us.

"But we ought always to thank God for you, brothers loved by the Lord, because from the beginning God chose you to be saved through the sanctifying work of the Spirit and through belief in the truth" (2 Thessalonians 2:13).

He is the vindication of Jesus Christ.

"Beyond all question, the mystery of godliness is great: He appeared in a body, was vindicated by the Spirit, was seen by angels, was preached among the nations, was believed on in the world, was taken up in glory" (1 Timothy 3:16).

He is our self-discipline.

"For God did not give us a spirit of timidity, but a spirit of power and of love and of self-discipline" (2 Timothy 1:7).

He helps us and guards that which is within us.

"Guard the good deposit that was entrusted to you—guard it with the help of the Holy Spirit who lives in us" (2 Timothy 1:14).

He washes us, He gives us rebirth, and He renews us.

"[H]e saved us, not because of righteous things we had done, but because of his mercy. He saved us through the washing of rebirth and renewal by the Holy Spirit" (Titus 3:5).

He distributes the gifts to us.

"God also testified to it by signs, wonders and various miracles, and gifts of the Holy Spirit distributed according to his will" (Hebrews 2:4).

He discloses the things of God to us.

"The Holy Spirit was showing by this that the way into the Most Holy Place had not yet been disclosed as long as the first tabernacle was still standing" (Hebrews 9:8).

It is he who preaches the gospel of God through us.

"It was revealed to them that they were not serving themselves but you, when they spoke of the things that have now been told you by those who have preached the gospel to you by the Holy Spirit sent from heaven. Even angels long to look into these things" (1 Peter 1:12).

He carries us along to speak the prophecies of God.

"For prophecy never had its origin in the will of man, but men spoke from God as they were carried along by the Holy Spirit" (2 Peter 1:21).

It is by the Spirit that we know God lives in us.

"Those who obey his commands live in him, and he in them. And this is how we know that he lives in us: We know it by the Spirit he gave us" (1 John 3:24).

"We know that we live in him and he in us, because he has given us of his Spirit" (1 John 4:13).

He is sent by God, and he is what is within us that cries out Abba, Father.

"Because you are sons, God sent the Spirit of his Son into our hearts, the Spirit who calls out, 'Abba, Father'" (Galatians 4:6).

CHAPTER 9

The Purpose

The twelfth chapter of 1 Corinthians is a very interesting read. Not only does it enumerate the nine gifts, but it gives us a pretty in-depth discussion of the body of Christ. It talks about how we are related one to another as a complex organism called the body of Christ made up of individual complex organisms. But it stresses that we are a part of one another, and furthermore it stresses that the gifts of the Holy Spirit are given to individual parts of this body for the common good of the entire body. We are very far from practicing this type of body ministry. But it is only with the Holy Spirit and his gifts (used by some for all and by all for some) that we will ever begin to see this body ministry come to pass.

Another keyword in this chapter is *manifestation*. The nine gifts are called the manifestation of the Holy Spirit. The word in the Greek used for *manifestation* actually means "the appearing of something." In other words, when we see the gifts function, we know the Holy Spirit is present. The converse of this is also true: no gifts, no assurance that the Holy Spirit is actually present. The church can be full of many great people who seem to love one another, the preaching can be great, the organist magnificent, and the liturgy well organized, but all of that can be done on a human level. When we see the gifts functioning for the common good, we know the Holy Spirit has shown up. Why do we know that, because that's what the Word says? If he's there, the gifts will be present, and in fact the gifts will show him to us. We will see, feel, and hear his presence through the gifts. The gifts are the manifestation (revelation) of the Holy Spirit.

Oftentimes people tend to overlook the Holy Spirit and his working in our lives because they believe the gifts, particularly speaking in tongues, causes divisions in fellowships. I would answer this using an example from the world. Whenever there is a tragedy involving guns, it is said that we must limit the use of guns because they kill. The counterargument to this statement is people kill, and sometimes they use guns.

The same is true about the Holy Spirit and any of his true manifestations. The Holy Spirit does not cause division; people do. If everything that causes division in a church were dismissed, no churches would have carpeting. People are naturally afraid of that which they do not understand, and fear often makes us attack. If attacked, people often defend, and others are made to take sides.

Several years ago, I was involved in a situation that might bring light to what I'm trying to say. There was a man in a nondenominational congregation who spoke in tongues. The gifts of the Holy Spirit were not a traditional part of this congregation, and respecting that, the man had never used his gifts publicly in that setting. The pastor knew, however, because in private conversation, he had asked this man's opinion about the gifts as one friend to another. At some point, several people came to the pastor and asked if this man could teach a Sunday school class. The man himself never solicited any type of leadership position in the congregation. After fielding several inquiries about a Sunday school class for this man, the pastor approached him and said in front of others that anyone who taught about speaking in tongues would never teach Sunday school in his church. The man smiled and said okay. However, the man's wife overheard the comment, and after considering it for a couple of weeks, she left the congregation and never returned. This was not the only reason his wife stopped going. For some time, she had felt judged by certain members, and in turn judged them. After she heard the pastor's comment, her feelings became almost paranoid in nature, and unable to reconcile how she felt with what she believed Christianity should be, she left. As word of the pastor's feelings spread, several other people also stopped attending that church. The man himself continued to go for some weeks but eventually joined his wife.

Now let me ask you the question: did the gift of tongues cause division? I think on several different levels, people caused the division. Tongues themselves were never taught, used publicly, or considered one way or the other. It was one man's proactive fear that started the division and perhaps the overreaction of others that finished it.

The pastor is a Bible-believing New Testament man, but in this situation, maybe he overlooked **1 Corinthians 14:39**, which says, **"Do not forbid speaking in tongues."**

In fact, the whole fourteenth chapter of 1 Corinthians might be one that the church overlooks. Chapter 14 could be overlooked because it follows 1 Corinthians 13, which could be, arguably, the most important chapter to the church in the whole Bible. Chapter 14 could also be overlooked because it does not fit well with either our theologies or our liturgies. Admittedly, it is a difficult chapter, and to reconcile it with our theologies and/or our liturgies, we would need to make difficult decisions or just ignore it. It's very possible that for the vast majority of us, ignorance of God's Word is our chosen path, either because it sits on the shelf and we don't read it at all or, if we do read it, we just accept those parts that are comfortable.

I challenge you to read 1 Corinthians 14 slowly and carefully and try to reconcile it with your current theology and mode of worship. Frequently when people do this, they come to the conclusion that it was written for different people in a different time and does not apply to us. Oftentimes these same people will pick out certain phrases and use the fourteenth chapter to discredit and dismiss the gifts of the Holy Spirit. Never should we dismiss any of the New Testament for a different time or a different people. When we do this, we are making the Word subjective—something it never is. We may not understand, but it is always and completely, objectively relevant to our life now. If we begin to pick and choose as it suits us, the Word is useless. If we could put our prejudices and paradigms aside for a moment and read the chapter objectively, we would see that it commands us to eagerly desire spiritual gifts and gives us guidelines in how to use them.

This then gives us a new dilemma. How could this possibly work in a congregation of 14,000—or 1,400 or even 140? Perhaps it could work in a congregation of 50, but even that seems large when the Word says, **"When you come together, each one has a hymn, or a word of instruction, a revelation, a tongue or an interpretation" (1 Corinthians 14:26).** This Scripture is not referring to Sunday school, midweek meetings, or anything else except our regular worship. And it definitely calls us to individual spiritual participation. It is such a far cry from the way we currently do church that we have to conclude that either the way we do church or the Word is wrong.

It is no wonder the gifts are not very prevalent in the church. The Devil has so constructed the way we do church that we are not much better than cattle being herded through a religious corral every Sunday and inoculated with our dose of spirituality for another week. The gifts are not more prevalent because we are not allowed to use them as they are supposed to be used.

I said earlier that the Holy Spirit has basically two jobs in this world: to protect us from the world, the flesh, and the Evil One and to show the world the true character of God. Included in showing the world the true character of God is body ministry. The true character of God is one of a triune nature: three separate parts that function independently but are actually one. I think we all would admit that there are many times we do not actually know which member— Father, Son, or Holy Spirit—is actually functioning in our lives at that moment. And furthermore, we do not even consider that it matters. That is how intimately entwined the Godhead is.

I believe the Holy Spirit's main job in his people is to bring about the same intimate entwining. If I'm right, Christianity is a failure, or at least the members are failing to achieve the maximum it has to offer.

Several Scriptures say point-blank that we are members of the body of Christ and should be as intimately connected to each other as your skin and flesh is to your skeleton. Among them are these:

"And God placed all things under his [Christ's] feet and appointed him to be head over everything for *the church, which is his body,* **the fullness of him who fills everything in every way" (Ephesians 1:22–24, italics mine).**

"Therefore each of you must put off falsehood and speak truthfully to his neighbor, *for we are all members of one body"* **(Ephesians 4:25, italics mine).**

"Now you are the body of Christ, **and each one of you is a part of it" (1 Corinthians 12:27, italics mine).**

I contend that Jesus was not sent by the Father for the salvation of our souls, nor was the Holy Spirit sent by Jesus to fill us with power. Those were benefits of the real purpose. The real purpose was for us to become one in the Godhead and to take back, by faith, this corrupt and fallen world. The Word hints of this when it says **in Ephesians 1:24, "... the church which is his body the fullness of him**

who fills everything in every way." What this Scripture is saying is that the church is the fullness of Christ and is to fill everything in every way with his character.

This theme is further carried in **Ephesians 3:9–11, "... and to make plain to everyone the administration of this mystery, which for ages past was kept hidden in God, who created all things. His intent was that now, through the church, the manifold wisdom of God should be made known to the rulers and authorities in the heavenly realms, and according to his eternal purpose which he accomplished in Christ Jesus our Lord."**

The mystery spoken of is that all who are made alive in Jesus Christ are one. The administration of this oneness mystery is that through this oneness, the rulers and authorities in heavenly realms shall be stripped of their power and through his body, Christ shall rule. Thy will be done on earth as it is in heaven. This has always been his *one* intended, eternal purpose. Everything else is an add-on.

This theme is amplified throughout Ephesians and perhaps begins to explain clearly our purpose and destiny. **Ephesians 1:9–10** says, **"And he made known to us the mystery of his will ... to bring all things in heaven and on earth together under one head, even Christ."** Truly, all things shall be brought under the head, but it is meant to happen though the works of the body.

God speaks to us in parables; there are huge meanings often in small phrases. An example of this, and also more to my point, can be found in **Ephesians 1:18–22:**

> **I pray also that the eyes of your heart may be enlightened in order that you may know the hope to which he has called you, the riches of**

his glorious inheritance in the saints, and his incomparably great power for us who believe. That power is like the working of his mighty strength, which he exerted in Christ when he raised him from the dead and seated him at his right hand in the heavenly realms, far above all rule and authority, power and dominion, and every title that can be given, not only in the present age but also in the one to come. And God placed all things under his feet and appointed him to be head over everything for the church, which is his body, the fullness of him who fills everything in every way.

In verse 18 he wants us to know of the hope of a redeemed earth that is our inheritance, and the bounty it provides. Then he speaks of the incomparable great power for us who believe. That power is given to us as a body to fulfill the hope of redeeming this earth for the glory of the Father. Then he tells us when this is to happen, *in this present age* and in the one to come.

But all of that is not the most exciting part of that body of Scripture. I don't think any of us would disagree with the Scripture that God exerted great power and raised Christ from the dead and put him far above all rule and authority, power and dominion, and every title that can be given. But here's where it gets exciting: where is Jesus? He is seated at the right hand of the Father. But where has all of this dominion and rule and authorities been placed? Under his feet! The feet are the lowest extremity of the body—the farthest from the head—but nonetheless they are part of the body. In this Scripture, God is telling us that any part of the body is above and has more authority than the rulers of this present world. And in fact, if we will open our eyes to it we are, as the body, rulers of this present world. But a ruler who will not rule does not rule.

"For in Christ all the fullness of the Deity lives in bodily form, and you have been given fullness in Christ, who is the head over every power and authority" (Colossians 2:9–10). Well, this Scripture pretty well sums it up. We simply need to ask the question, What is the bodily form of Christ? The church is the obvious answer. Well then, the church possesses the fullness of all of the Deity, because it says we have been given all of the fullness that is in Christ. And if we have received his complete fullness (as he is head over every power and authority) we, as his body, are over every power and authority.

Here's the problem: we are not a body. We are basically a group of individuals who meet together, around common beliefs, doing certain things so we can feel good about ourselves.

Now let's contrast that with the first-century church as it is described in Acts:

> All the believers were together and had everything in common. Selling their possessions and goods, they gave to anyone as he had need. Every day they continued to meet together in the temple courts. They broke bread in their homes and ate together with glad and sincere hearts, praising God and enjoying the favor of all the people. And the Lord added to their number daily those who were being saved. (Acts 2:44–47)

> All the believers were one in heart and mind. No one claimed that any of his possessions was his own, but they shared everything they had. With great power the apostles continued to testify to the resurrection of the Lord Jesus,

and much grace was upon them all. There were no needy persons among them. For from time to time those who owned lands or houses sold them, brought the money from the sales and put it at the apostles' feet, and it was distributed to anyone as he had need. (Acts 4:32–35)

Wow—is it any wonder the church has such little power? We are so far removed from what the first-century church stood for that we can't even imagine getting there if we wanted to.

The church as we know it resembles an American corporation more than it does the first-century church. You have your board of directors, the elders; you have your CEO, the pastor; and you have your balance sheet, fueled by income resources such as collections, bake sales, and car washes. You have your expenditures, the hired shepherds who need their guaranteed salaries; your support staff and their guaranteed salaries; and your facilities and its overhead. The bigger you are, the more successful you appear. It is a machine that is fueled by making sure people get a regular dose of their feel-good Christianity.

If what I am saying is true, we've been sold a horrible bill of goods called religion. But then again, maybe it didn't take much to sell it to us because it's so easy. Maybe we prefer to be like Ananias and Sapphira, living a lie rather than dying to self and becoming like the sacrificing unified Christians of the first century.

Everything about us is much the same as the world. We make our money and spend it like the world, we watch the same TV shows and go to the same movies, we have the same illnesses and go to the same doctors, and our moral outlooks are similar, as we can tell by the divorce and infidelity rates being the same as the world's. I realize these are hard words, but they are no harder than the words

Jesus spoke to the religious peoples of his day and how he warned people that their righteousness must be more than that of the scribes and Pharisees. It's no harder than the Word, which tells us we are the salt of the earth but that if we lose our saltiness, we are less than worthless. It is no harder than the admonition to "love not the world or the things of the world for if we do the love of the Father is not in us."

If we're honest, I think we will easily see that the American church is nowhere near what Jesus envisioned for his people. I know I am being a hypocrite by pointing that out. First, I'm right smack-dab in the middle of the problem, and second, I don't know what to do about it. I have no answers. I can't even imagine how the first-century church would function in today's world. But maybe there is something we can do. Maybe we can pray a prayer like, "Father, I pray that you may open the eyes of my heart that I may know the hope to which you have called me and the riches of your glorious inheritance that you have in me, and that I may comprehend your incomparable great power released in me when I believe."

Maybe we can do something else, too. Maybe if we stop playing feel-good religion and start to get real with God, he will get real to us. He really doesn't care how big the church we go to is, how great the sermon the pastor teaches, how they love one another (on Sunday morning), or about any of the other feel-good ways we express our spirituality. If you really want to know what impresses God, find the eight to twelve people he has picked out for you to become connected with—people with whom you meet on a regular basis and speak godly, prophetic wisdom into each other's lives; people who are so intimate with each other that most of the dark places have light shed into them. They are people of the truth who will risk your love for them by speaking the truth into your life. And most of all, they are people who will gladly receive truth spoken to their own lives. Look for them; they are out there looking for you.

I know what the promises are for us who believe. We have covered two of these promises: the salvation of our souls and the infilling of us by God's Spirit. There are three more to go, and that is really what this book is about. It is important to realize that when God talks about believing, he means believing the promises. Receiving Jesus Christ as our Lord and Savior is a promise. Being baptized in his Holy Spirit is a promise. These are not the ends; they are promises that lead and enable us to believe even more promises, such as a healed body, a prosperous soul, and a godly character. But as we go on and speak of these promises, let us never forget they are promises. The Father sent the Son, who, after his death and resurrection, sent the Holy Spirit to redeem a fallen world system from the Evil One. That is simply and precisely why he saved us and filled us with his power and authority, so that we as his body are equipped to do the work of wrestling the world from the hands of Satan and his demonic helpers.

"For our struggle is not against flesh and blood, but against the rulers, against the authorities, against the powers of this dark world and against the spiritual forces of evil in the heavenly realms" (Ephesians 6:12).

CHAPTER 10

Anyone Seen My Body?

I know at the beginning of this book, I promised simplicity, and somehow in some places it seems to be very complex. But what I really promised was that God spoke to us in simple ways. It is our hearing that complicates things. We are so programmed to believe certain things in certain ways that we interpret what God is saying from those positions.

An example would be our position in God. We are programmed to believe that when we accept Jesus Christ, he lives in us. How we see this, then, is Jesus somehow living in a small place in our heart. Big us, little Jesus. I'm not saying that there is not some scriptural reference to Jesus living in our hearts. What I am saying is that there is a much bigger scriptural picture that God has painted but because of our Jesus-living-in-our-hearts theology, we miss it.

This bigger picture is called the body of Christ. In this picture you would see Christ as a head having a body, and somewhere within that body made up of thousands would be you and me. Big God, little me. And furthermore, this body is under the head (Christ) seated next to the Father in heaven. I understand the difficulty of believing that we are currently in heaven ministering to earth, but that is the reality that the Scriptures give us in **Ephesians 2:6—"And God raised us up with Christ and seated us with him in the heavenly**

realms in Christ Jesus'—and **Colossians 3:1—"Since, then, you have been raised with Christ, set your hearts on things above, where Christ is seated at the right hand of God."**

In the first scenario, we are earthly and reaching to the heavenly. In this second scenario, we are heavenly reaching to the earth. Whichever scenario we believe becomes our reality. When we believe the first, we are basically a lone ranger, constantly reaching out to God, often as a beggar. When we believe the second, we are a small part of something much bigger that surrounds us, keeps us, and protects us. It magnifies and empowers our prayers, for we are no longer praying to God; now we are praying from God.

Look at the next three Scriptures and particularly the highlighted parts and you perhaps will begin to see what I'm talking about. It is not big me, little God; rather, it is little me, big God.

"Now *you are the body of Christ,* and each one of you is a part of it" (1 Corinthians 12:27, italics mine).

"Let us fix our eyes on *Jesus,* the author and perfecter of our faith, who for the joy set before him endured the cross, scorning its shame, and *sat down at the right hand of the throne of God"* (Hebrews 12:2, italics mine).

Since, then, *you have been raised with Christ,* set your hearts on things above, *where Christ is seated at the right hand of God"* (Colossians 3:1–2, italics mine).

"Christ is the head of the church, his body, of which he is the Savior" (Ephesians 5:23). This Scripture clearly points out that Christ is the head and we are his body. The *we* is a corporate *we.* I am not the body of Christ, simply a small part of that body. How important a part depends upon how much I understand and believe. To illustrate this point, let's play a word picture game. We have pointed out that Christ is the head of the body and also that he is seated at the right hand of the Father. Now imagine a head sitting on the throne next to the Father with no body—just Jesus' head. Maybe even imagine the head turning and talking to the Father. Remember, no body. It kind of makes a ridiculous and somewhat scary picture. But if we follow Scripture through, that is exactly what our theology would draw.

Usually when we think of Jesus, we probably think of a TV or movie character with long hair and a long, flowing robe covering his body. Never or at least rarely will we ever see ourselves as a part of that body. Let's now play another word picture game. Remember the game Where Is Waldo? There's a huge crowd of tiny cartoon figures. Somewhere in that crowd is Waldo, and your job is to find him. Well, let's play a variation of that game. Again, imagine the head of Christ seated at the right hand of the Father, only this time he has a body. I'm willing to bet that your mind went straight to the flowing robes. But instead of the flowing robes, his body is completely made up of faces—millions and millions of faces. The neck is faces, the torso is faces, the arms and legs and even the feet are all made up of the faces of real people. Now, your job is to find your face. Somewhere interspersed among all those faces is yours. Are we beginning to understand who we are in the real substantial body of Christ? Big God, little me. This is not to at all undermine our importance in and to the body, but it is to bring into focus our place in Christ. It is not Christ and me, it is very much Christ and we.

The average human body has about .2 mg of gold in it. For those of you who do not understand metric measurements any better than I do, that's .000007 of an ounce. It's almost nothing, and yet, if we do not have it, our muscles will ache and our equilibrium will be off. This is simply to illustrate how important each part of the body is to the overall health and function of the whole body. **"From**

Christ, the whole body, joined and held together by every supporting ligament, grows and builds itself up in love, as each part does its work" (Ephesians 4:16). We must first know that we are part of the body before we can begin to be part of the body. It is by faith.

Okay, let me try to illustrate this point in another way. I want you to pound a nail into a board. It's not a particularly difficult task, except that I want you to use just your head. Any way you want to do this is fine with me: you can pound it in with your head or you can use a hammer in your mouth, but the only part of your body you can use is your head. Let me know how that works for you. Okay, that did not work, so let us try something else. Lay the board down and lay the nail on top of it. Now with your mind, think the nail into the board. Got a headache yet? Okay, now take the hammer, take the nail, and pound the nail into the board using your arm, wrist, and hand. That's not a particularly difficult project if you have some degree of skill and coordination.

My point with this ridiculous exercise is simply that the head needs the body to function in most things. We pray to God and ask him to do things, but He is the head and has constructed us as the body for a reason. Think of it in simple terms: the head directs, the body does. No single part of the body is much good unless it works intimately with the other parts of the body. In simple terms, God does the thinking and directs us to do the doing. Often all we have to do is speak forth the Word in faith.

Here's the problem: generally speaking in the American church, one part of the body has absolutely no true connection to other parts of the body. Remember the discussion about the eight to twelve people in your life? These people, who speak God into your life and are intimately connected to you, are what keep you connected to the rest of the body, and more important, to the head. Without them you will suffer atrophy and die and could even affect the rest of the body as a gangrenous infection.

To make a point, I might facetiously describe Christ as having the disease amyotrophic lateral sclerosis (ALS) or, as it is commonly called, Lou Gehrig's disease. This is a disease in which basically the mind functions but the body does not respond to its signals. Sounds to me a lot like how we as the corporate body respond to Christ.

Let us clear up a point. I'm not talking about you and Jesus. I'm not talking about you and the Jesus you visit in your prayer closet. I am sure that relationship is secure and stable. I am well aware that Christianity is made up of a personal relationship with the triune God, and I am also aware that almost a total emphasis is put upon this relationship. But I am equally aware that besides this personal relationship, Christianity is a corporate responsibility. God has chosen to describe this corporate responsibility to us as a body connected to a head. Every single cell in the body is somehow connected to the head, and if the connection is lost, the cell will die. Sometimes we confuse this connection to the head as the beginning and end of our experience with God, and we forget that it is only through many connections with others that we are actually connected to the head. **"From Christ, the whole body, joined and held together by every supporting ligament, grows and builds itself up in love, as each part does its work" (Ephesians 4:16).**

I've spent quite a bit of ink and paper trying to convince you that the real purpose for us being saved is to bring about the kingdom of God by being a corporate body. And yet I'm well aware that even Paul had trouble understanding the functioning of this corporate body. He says in **Ephesians 5:32, "This is a profound mystery—but I am talking about Christ and the church."**

So instead of trying to explain a mystery, let's talk about why we have a purpose. God created Adam and Eve to live in a paradise; they did not believe God and sold their birthright, this paradise into the hands of the Evil One. Ever since then, he has controlled not only this earth (paradise) but also the hearts of men. After a few attempts to redeem this situation failed, God finally sent his Son to be the new Adam. This new Adam destroyed the works of the Devil and made it possible for the hearts of man to be redeemed. But the real purpose of this redeemed man is to through faith wrestle the control of this earth from the Evil One, and to redeem our birthright heaven on earth. But why does this earth, this world, need redemption?

CHAPTER 11

The Evil Empire

This chapter is about what happened to this earth under the control of the Devil. There is a line from the movie *Gladiator* in which General Maximus is about to have the epic battle. They have sent surrender terms to the enemy, but they would not surrender and General Maximus said something to the effect of, "I hate it when an enemy doesn't know he is defeated." The same could be said for the Devil, for he is defeated but likewise the saying could be turned around. God could be saying of us, "I hate it when my people do not know they are victorious." I find it ironic that we are still having the same conversations with the Devil in our minds. We are still accepting his solutions as truth and thereby rejecting God's solutions. We continue to believe the lie no matter how preposterous and reject the truth no matter how simple.

God created the earth to be a perfect paradise for man. In this paradise all of man's needs would be taken care of. I do not think we can fully appreciate the perfection of this paradise, for we have never lived in anything but a fallen world. Imagine a world in which there is no death, where nothing ever rots or has an offensive smell. Imagine a world in which there is no sickness or poverty. That is the environment in which God intended man to live—in which Adam and Eve did live until they questioned God and believed the lie and handed the world over to the Devil.

There are three Scriptures that when considered together paint a pretty clear picture of what our relationship in the world and to the world should be. The first Scripture to consider is **1 John 5:19,** which says, **"[T]he whole world is under the control of the evil one."**

That Scripture tells us who has control in this world.

The second Scripture to consider **is John 10:10: "The thief comes only to steal and kill and destroy."**

This Scripture tells us categorically that the Devil's one and only purpose is destruction. Something else to consider with the combination of the two Scriptures above is that if the Evil One is in control of this world as the Word says, then this world must be evil. And even when something looks good, it will ultimately turn out to be evil. That brings us to the third Scripture, **James 4:4: "You adulterous people, don't you know that friendship with the world is hatred toward God? Anyone who chooses to be a friend of the world becomes an enemy of God."**

God cannot and will not sponsor evil. That is why he gives us such a stern warning in James 4:4. I do not believe that we have been properly taught how completely corrupted this world is. Nor have we been properly taught that we may be in this world but it is absolutely necessary that we not be of it.

How evil is this world? It is as absolutely evil as the Devil. People say to me, "But God made the world." And I answer, "That is true, but from the moment the world was handed to the Devil, it became corrupt, and within a single generation, we have a brother killing a brother. Within a few generations man had fallen so far and the world had become so evil that God found it necessary to clean the earth of both." As it turned out, this was only a temporary solution, for evil was still present.

Sun-tzu was a Chinese general and military strategist who said, "Know your enemy and know yourself, and you will always be victorious." I think if we were to amend this slightly, it would be a perfect saying for where we are. "Know your enemy, know yourself, and know your God, and you will always be victorious."

Now let us converse a little bit about our enemy and what he has done to God's beautiful earth. First of all, the Devil is not a creator—never has been and never will be. He only takes that which God has created and subverts it to evil. And trust me, if he is allowed to have a hand in something, no matter how good it appears on the surface, it is evil.

Probably the most important thing to know about the Devil is that he is a liar. **"He [the Devil] was a murderer from the beginning, not holding to the truth, for there is no truth in him. When he lies, he speaks his native language, for he is a liar and the father of lies" (John 8:44).** Notice that not only is he described as a liar, but that it is said that no truth is in him. It may seem to be the truth, but if it is of the world, it will ultimately be a lie, and its purpose is to destroy.

The attack upon us from the Devil and his demons is relentless. We must constantly be diligently aware of these attacks. There are countless ways in which they intrude into our lives. **1 John 2:16** warns us of three of the ways that the Evil One attacks us: **lust of the eyes, lust of the flesh, and boastful pride of life.** The Word tells us quite plainly in 1 John 2 that these things do not come from God but rather from the world, and we have already established who controls the world.

Briefly described, the lust of the eyes is a desire for things, the lust of the flesh is desire for pleasure, and the boastful pride of life is desire for position. If we look all the way back to the garden, we can see that the Devil tempted Eve through the lust of the eyes, the lust of the flesh, and the boastful pride of life. **"When the woman saw that the fruit of the tree was good for food and pleasing to the eye, and also desirable for gaining wisdom, she took some and ate it" (Genesis 3:6).** Eve saw that the fruit was good for food (lust for things), pleasing to the eye (lust for pleasure), and desirable for gaining wisdom equal to God's (lust for position).

These are basically the same temptations that the Devil brought to Jesus after his sojourn in the desert, and our response should be exactly like his. With every temptation, Jesus responded with the Word of God. Always remember the Devil does not have a lot of tricks, but he does use the same ones very effectively over and over, and we fall for them again and again. That is, until we begin to know and use the Word of God.

The Devil and his demons are constantly speaking at us to get us to do their bidding. But they are not the only voices. The world and the flesh are also deeply interested in our destruction. When these voices are obeyed, they are either self-gratifying or self-destructive, and in most cases they are both. When they are denied, they become loud, demanding, and relentless. They use fear, condemnation, shame, and maybe most of all, self-desire as motivators. The world lies to us, the flesh disappoints us, and the Devil condemns us.

Each of these three things—the world, the flesh, and the Devil—has its particular way of worming into our lives. The world intrudes primarily through our eyes, the flesh primarily through our faculties of emotion and reason, and the Devil through our heart, using unredeemed areas such as unforgiveness, hatred, unconfessed sin, generational sin, and so on.

As each of them may have a primary point of intrusion into our lives, there is a primary way for us to deal with each of them.

We escape the corruption that is in the world by faith. **"[E]veryone born of God overcomes the world. And this is the victory that has overcome the world, even our faith"** (1 John 5:4).

We escape the flesh through the cross. **"[W]e know that our old self [our flesh] was crucified with him so that the body of sin might be done away with, that we should no longer be slaves to sin"** (Romans 6:6).

And we overcome the Devil by our word and the blood of Christ. **"[T]hey overcame him [the Devil] by the blood of the lamb and the word of their testimony"** (Revelation 12:11).

The last thing we want to do is ignore the Devil as if he doesn't exist. The Word tells us to resist and he shall flee. It is tough to resist him if you ignore him. Ignoring the Devil is like ignoring a warning that a flood is rushing toward you. Ignorance will not stop the waters but will leave you ill prepared to deal with them. I have friends who have been in the Lord about as long as I have, and one time in a conversation I mentioned that I probably talk to the Devil as much as I talk to God. They were somewhat taken aback, and both said they don't pay any attention to the Devil, for he is defeated. Yet in their lives and in the lives of their children, we see a great deal of defeat. Sickness, poverty, and less than victorious lives are all products of the Evil One.

In my conversations with the Devil, I remind him (using Scripture) that he is defeated and that what he is whispering in my ear at that moment is a lie and doesn't line up with the Word of God. I rebuke him and tell him and all his evil ones to take their lies somewhere else. I then thank Jesus Christ for his victory and remind myself of his promises. Sometimes it works.

When it doesn't work, it usually ends up being sin. But even then, the Devil does not have to win if we believe the promises.

"But if anybody does sin, we have one who speaks to the Father in our defense—Jesus Christ, the Righteous One. He is the atoning sacrifice for our sins" (1 John 1:9). "If we confess our sins, he is faithful and just and will forgive us our sins and purify us from all unrighteousness" (1 John 2:1–2). Sin is never good, but do not believe the lie that sin separates you from God. Remember the example of Adam and Eve: when they were disobedient, it did not change God's attitude toward them; it changed their attitude toward God. God still came looking for fellowship with them, but they hid from him. If we do not repent when we fall short, we will find ourselves sooner or later hiding in our sin from God.

"'The thief comes only to steal and kill and destroy; I have come that they may have life, and have it to the full'" (John 10:10). This Scripture tells us a great deal not only about the Devil and God but also about us. It calls the Devil the thief and tells us his primary purpose is to destroy. Then it tells us that God's purpose for us is life to abundance. But it asks us, why do we settle for less than his best? To me the only answer possible is that we are listening to the liar instead of to the truth.

The Word tells us to know that God is and that he rewards those who seek him. But we must also know what the Devil is, and he is a stealer from those who ignore him.

Here are five tools to help us overcome the Evil One:

1) Get dressed. **"Put on the full armor of God that you may be able to stand firm against the schemes of the devil"** (Ephesians 6:11).

2) Get knowledge. **"His divine power has given us everything we need for life and godliness through our knowledge of him who called us by his own glory and goodness. Through these he has given us his very great and precious promises, so that through them you may participate in the divine nature and escape the corruption in the world caused by evil desires"** (2 Peter 1:3–4).

3) Speak forth. **"[T]hey overcame him by the blood of the lamb and the word of their testimony"** (Revelation 12:11).

4) Submit and resist. **"[S]ubmit yourselves, then, to God. Resist the devil, and he will flee from you"** (James 4:7).

5) Finally stand. **"[S]tand firm then, with the belt of truth buckled around your waist with the breastplate of righteousness in place"** (Ephesians 6:14).

This simple chapter is not intended to be an encyclopedia of victory over the evil forces that come against us. There are plenty of great books out there dedicated to just that purpose. This was simply intended to be a thumbnail sketch of both the Devil's evil and our ways to achieve victory.

CHAPTER 12

Our Kingdom

But you are a chosen people, a royal priesthood, a holy nation, a people belonging to God, that you may declare the praises [excellencies] of him who called you out of darkness into his wonderful light.

—1 Peter 2:9

According to the above Scripture, he called us out of something and into something else. Why? For what purpose? The phrase *that you may declare* is better translated in the King James Version as "shown forth" or "demonstrate." Demonstrate what? Well, the Word says "the praise of him." The word *praise* should be translated as "virtue," literally meaning "manliness or strength." So in other words, you move from an evil kingdom to a righteous one to show forth the strength of our Father to bring forth righteousness and dispel evil through redeemed man.

"But seek first his kingdom and his righteousness, and all these things shall be given to you as well" (Matthew 6:33).

My two children tend to take their jobs very seriously, and I have often quoted the verse above to them as a balance. But one night the Holy Spirit awoke me (Has he ever done that to you? It really gets your attention) and told me that although what I was saying to them was first seek him, that's not what the Scripture says. In fact, I had to get up and look at it. And this started me off on an amazing journey.

Actually, the Scripture says seek his kingdom! As I began to look, I was surprised to find how many times his kingdom is referred to in the New Testament, especially by Jesus. I do not recall ever hearing a sermon or teaching on seeking his kingdom as it is taught in the Word.

What does the phrase *his kingdom* mean? It does not mean a place; rather, correctly translated, it means a reign or a rule. And it is quite clear it does not mean something in the future; rather it means to bring it forth now.

"... and from Jesus Christ ... who has made us to be a kingdom and priests unto His God and Father" (Revelation 1:5–6).

A kingdom and priests are two separate things. He did not say priests in his kingdom; rather, he said *a* kingdom and priests. The priesthood of the believer is a great teaching, but it has more to do with our authority to call forth redemption for others—that is, intercession, binding, and loosing. But the kingdom has everything to do with bringing forth God's rule on this earth with the authority and power he has vested in us, his body.

What we are seeing is two kingdoms with very few similarities. The earth is a kingdom of time and space. It can be measured and has its limits in both time and space. The kingdom of God, on the other hand, has neither time nor space. It is as real as—in fact more real than—the kingdom of the earth but cannot be measured in time or space. That is why it is so hard for physicists to believe in God, for everything they do is measured in time and space. We have to find the beginning so we can begin measuring and make sense out of everything because of our measurements. But this is where we go wrong with God and his kingdom. They have neither time nor space.

The kingdom of God is not a place, nor does it take up space, and it is not limited by time or space. I'm very hesitant to try to explain something that occupies neither time nor space. The closest I can come is to say that in our experience, it would be a little like a thought. Because we are finite and both God and his kingdom are infinite, we simply cannot fully understand. I can hear people say that's foolishness because God's Word describes him as a person and his kingdom as a place. A case in point would be **John 18:36**, which says, **"Jesus said, my kingdom is not of this world. If it were, my servants would fight to prevent my arrest by the Jews. But now my kingdom is from another place."** The word translated "place" from the Greek is *hence*. This is a slippery little word that can be translated "place" but is not completely defined by that translation. When used in the context above, the word would better be translated as "of something completely different." As far as time is concerned, when God tells us that to him a day is like a thousand years, he is simply telling us he does not measure by time. God gave us time so that we could make sense out of this universe. The very word *eternal* implies "without time."

It's important for us to begin to understand outside of time and space because the Devil uses the confines of time and space to control us. It is only within the confines of what we can see and touch that our finite minds can understand. However, as we go beyond the finite and begin to understand the measurelessness of God and his kingdom, we will become less finite and more infinite, and that is where the "walk of faith" begins.

As I said, it is nearly impossible to explain a heaven with no time or space. It goes beyond our minds to understand anything beyond that which we can see and touch. I have heard our existence described as a snow globe, with this universe being the inside and eternity being the outside. The trouble with this definition is that the snow globe is a thick glass enclosure, and that which separates us from the kingdom of God does not really exist. Okay, now I have confused even myself. I also have heard it described as a veil. In this definition, the veil is actually over our senses, and although the kingdom of God is all around us, we cannot perceive it because of this veil.

There are three stories that somewhat illustrate how closely we exist to the kingdom of God. The first story might be the best. It is the story of Enoch, who visited with God regularly and one day just went for a walk with God and stepped through the curtain. I have always confessed I want this to be my experience and my wife always says, "Please leave a note." Then there's the story of Elijah, who was out jogging and was picked up by a chariot of fire and disappeared. But my favorite story is that of the first New Testament martyr, Stephen, who saw into the kingdom of God and was so amazed, he forgot to duck.

God alone is described as omnipresent (present in all places at all times), and yet with our carnal senses we perceive him nowhere. Do I need to fully understand a God of no time or space? I sure hope not, for I have not even begun to understand it myself, and that might be the very point. Because the Holy Spirit has given me a revelation of a God I cannot understand, I no longer try to understand him. Nor do I try to know him, feel him, or see him. All I can do is commit to believe him and hope that he will find that commitment pleasing and overwhelm me.

As I try to view spirituality pragmatically, the above is probably the most mystical paragraph you will ever hear from me. If indeed the entire paragraph tends to be mystical, the "commit to believe » part is entirely pragmatic. The secret of the kingdom is to know the promises and to believe (have faith in) them. As **Hebrews 11:6** tells us, faith is the only way to please God. **"And without faith it is impossible to please God, because anyone who comes to him must believe that he exists and that he rewards those who earnestly seek him."** This Scripture is the signature Scripture about faith. It gives us great insight into the character and simplicity of God: the character of God because it points out that he is a giver and the simplicity of God because he points out that it takes faith to understand that he exists and he exists as this giver. There is a problem with the Scripture, however, and that is in the last part that says "those who earnestly seek him." Sometimes people get entirely lost when they see the word *earnestly*. Some translations use the word *diligent*, but actually, neither word is in the Greek; rather they are implied, in the opinion of the translators. I don't have a problem with the words themselves; it is with our interpretation of what they mean. Oftentimes I have heard people say that to please God, they must spend a lot of time in prayer, go to church, or a million other legalistic ordinances. Actually what the Scripture is saying is that when we believe God exists and are continually practicing faith, God rewards us. It is the diligence and earnestness of our practicing faith that pleases God to release to us the reward—that is, whatever we have asked for.

This theme is further amplified by **2 Corinthians 5:7**, which says, **"We live by faith, not by sight."** As the Scripture implies, our life is to be lived totally dependent on God for our existence. Further, **"Jesus, the author and perfecter of our faith" (<u>Hebrews 12:2</u>),** points out that Jesus is both the author and perfecter of our faith, and therefore any of the pious acts we may do does not affect it. **"The life I live in the body, I live by faith in the Son of God" (Galatians 2:20)** also shouts this theme.

The Word says it is impossible to please God without faith, but it is also impossible to understand the kingdom without faith. Faith is the key that unlocks the door to the kingdom. It is beyond the scope of human reason and understanding to comprehend the kingdom of God. It is only as we view the kingdom through the faithful eyes of Jesus that we can begin to comprehend that which exists outside time and space, that which creates from nothing, and that which promises us so much. That is why Jesus is called the author and perfecter.

> **... who through faith conquered kingdoms, administered justice, and gained what was promised; who shut the mouths of lions, quenched the fury of the flames, and escaped the edge of the sword; whose weakness was turned to strength; and who became powerful in battle and routed foreign armies. Women received back their dead, raised to life again. Others were tortured and refused to be released, so that they might gain a better resurrection. (Hebrews 11:33–35)**

The practitioners mentioned in the above Scripture did not conquer kingdoms or do any of the other things mentioned the first time God spoke to them. In fact, many of them failed and succeeded only after trial and error. This faith I speak of is the fruit of faith as spoken of in Galatians 5:22. This fruit of faithfulness as with all fruit does not appear fully developed but rather grows with practice. I have heard faith described as a muscle that is strengthened only through use, and if it is not used, it atrophies. The same person said perhaps we should not try to determine the destiny of a nation until we can pray successfully for a good parking place at Walmart. God is equally interested in both.

Faith is a simple thing. Simply put, it is just believing the Word of God. Not the Word of God as a whole—not like saying, "Of course I believe the Bible." Rather, I mean believing one verse, even just one word or one promise as it is spoken to us by the Holy Spirit. I mean believing so much that after we hear it, we allow this new knowledge to change our whole thought patterns and actions. Faith makes it possible to follow **Romans 12:2**, which says, **"Do not conform any longer to the pattern of this world, but be transformed by the renewing of your mind."** This in turn begins the fulfillment of **2 Corinthians 3:18**: **"And we, who with unveiled faces all reflect the Lord's glory, are being transformed into his likeness with ever increasing glory, which comes from the Lord, who is the Spirit."** Faith is wonderful, and God's plan of faith is simply wonderful.

Many years ago, I learned to fly a plane, and although I never got instrument certified, I was taught certain basics. One of them was to always believe your instruments. Many pilots have crashed in heavy weather over the years because they did not believe that they were flying level even though their instruments told them they were. Adjusting the course according to how they felt resulted in their crashing and more often than not their death. Faith is like that instrument that tells us we are flying level. The world, the flesh, and the Devil tell us we must adjust our course. They use phrases such as *Don't be foolish, Everybody knows,* and *God gave them to us to use* to try to persuade us that the worldly way is the correct and sensible way. They will do whatever they need to do to persuade us to make a decision based on emotion and reason rather than faith in whatever the Holy Spirit tells us. They will tell you that the Scripture that says friendship with the world makes you an enemy of God does not mean what it says and does not say what it means. And whoever believes the world's lies will be much like the pilot not believing his altimeter, and sooner or later they will crash and burn.

- As we begin to appropriate small words of Scripture as our own, two things are likely to happen: the Devil, our flesh, and the world will try to steal the Word, and if they can't do that, then they will try to dilute it. Only full strength produces full results. The other thing that happens is that God almost always immediately gives us an opportunity to work the Word. Faith without action is dead. The Word is alive and active.

We must be careful, though, not to confuse the action with faith for that produces legalism. Faith is simply believing the Word, and the action is a result of that belief. For instance, not going to a doctor is not faith or an act of faith; it is rather a result of faith. The faith is believing the Scriptures that say God has healed us once for all. And why would we go to a doctor when we are healthy? However, if we confuse not going to a doctor with faith, we will be loath to go to the doctor. It will actually seem like a sin. Rather, I do not go to a doctor because faith has made me well, and I have no need. But if the Father asks me to visit the doctor, I am surely free to do so.

Another example is in the area of giving. People confuse tithing with faith. Tithing is an act. Faith is a belief. Faith is believing that God is and that he is a rewarder. It is not our action that gets us rewarded; it is our belief. Tithing is an act, and we never please God by our acts, only by our belief. **"And without faith it is impossible to please God" (Hebrews 11:6). "All of us have become like one who is unclean, and all our righteous acts are like filthy rags" (Isaiah 64:6).** The receiving is by faith; the giving is by obedience. According to the following Scriptures, only faith produces righteousness. **Romans 1:5 says, "... the obedience that comes from faith,"** and then **Romans 6:16** says, **"... to obedience, which leads to righteousness."** Our obedience is righteous only when it originates in faith. No action is righteous in and of itself. It is only when we are told by the person of the Holy Spirit; then our obedience to that word is credited to us as righteous. **David says the same thing when he speaks of the blessedness of the man to whom God credits righteousness apart from works (Romans 4:6).** When we confuse faith and works—or, put another way, belief and actions—we will find that we will be condemning ourselves when we don't act certain ways and will be judging others if they don't act in certain ways.

Instead of considering what faith is, let us think of what it does. Faith creates. When we exercise our faith, **"Nothing will be impossible for us" (Matthew 17:20).** Remember, the Word of God is simply preposterous and preposterously simple.

CHAPTER 13

Counterfeit

However, as it is written:

"No eye has seen,
no ear has heard,
no mind has conceived"
what God has prepared for those who love him
but God has revealed it to us by his Spirit

The Spirit searches all things, even the deep things
of God. For who among men knows the thoughts of
a man except the man's spirit within him? In the
same way no one knows the thoughts of God except
the Spirit of God. We have not received the spirit of
the world but the Spirit who is from God, that we
may understand what God has freely given us. This
is what we speak, not in words taught us by human
wisdom but in words taught by the Spirit, expressing
spiritual truths in spiritual words. The man without
the Spirit does not accept the things that come from the
Spirit of God, for they are foolishness to him, and he
cannot understand them, because they are spiritually
discerned. The spiritual man makes judgments about

> *all things, but he himself is not subject to any man's judgment:*
>
> *"For who has known the mind of the Lord that he may instruct him?"*
> *But we have the mind of Christ.*
> **—1 Corinthians 2:9ind**

God promised us three things to fulfill all our needs and desires. They are health, holiness, and prosperity, and they are free for simply believing. The Devil, on the other hand, has converted these three into the world's offering, which will always cost us, sometimes in pain, usually in money, and always driven by fear. The Devil's counterfeits of health, holiness, and prosperity are science, religion, and commerce.

The Devil cannot create; he only converts, taking that which God has created so that we may live life in abundance and converting it to evil, sometimes disguised as good. Take this world, for instance. God created it as a paradise, but from the moment the Evil One gained control over it, he has brought death, destruction, disease, wars, and poverty.

We know from Scripture's 1 John 3:1 and James 4:4 that there is a schism between God and the world. But we also have Scriptures such as **Psalm 24:1,** which says, **"The earth is the Lord's, and the fullness thereof; the world, and they that dwell therein."** That seems to indicate that God rules this earth. Then we have **Psalm 115:16: "The highest heavens belong to the Lord, but the earth he has given to man."** That clearly says he gave earth to man.

A friend of mine tells a story that kind of puts the whole thing into perspective. One day he was making a auto trip of about an hour and a half, and he thought it would be a good time to spend some high-quality time with his heavenly Father. So he cleared off the seat next to him and prepared to have a conversation. As it was a gorgeous day and everything around him looked so beautiful, he began to comment to his Father about what a beautiful earth he had created. Just about that same moment, a large billboard caught his eye. The billboard was advertising an adult novelty store and strip club. And very clearly he heard God say, "Yes, I created a beautiful earth, but look what man has done to it." The rest of the trip home, God showed him how man has corrupted God's earth.

God's way and the world's way have one thing in common: they both require faith. If we are to believe God and his promises, the only substance and evidence that we have is faith (Hebrews 11:1 NKJV). I believe the Devil's counterfeits take more faith than the kingdom's promises. To believe the counterfeits, we must ignore their overwhelming failures and convince ourselves that they will work for us. We must overlook the lies and somehow convince ourselves that it's not all a lie. But not only does science, religion, and commerce lie to us, but their purpose in lying to us is to rob, steal from, and kill us (John 10:10). In the process of robbing, stealing, and killing us, they attempt to render the Word of God useless and foolish.

An example of this is the so-called science of evolution. It attempts to explain the beginnings of man and dismisses any explanation outside its own as ignorant superstition. Evolution's basic premise is that somehow, somewhere, there was a basic substance, and from that, all creation was formed. It fails to explain where the basic substance comes from and can't provide any true documentation of the ongoing process of evolution or any real evolutionary evidence from the past. And yet we believe in this foolishness or at least allow it to be taught to our children. Why? Most likely because it is called science, and we are told that if we believe anything else, we are superstitious and ignorant. Well, who wants to be superstitious and ignorant? Me!

You see, it requires way too much faith to believe the theory of evolution. It just has too many holes in it, and more important, it categorically rejects and denies God's simple explanation for the beginning of this universe. Science in its attempt to be its own god must deny the existence of any other god and must create a wisdom separate from any other god. This scripture passage is central to our understanding of how we are to live in the world and still be of the kingdom: **"For the wisdom of this world is foolishness in God's sight" (1 Corinthians 3:19).**

God's simple explanation of the beginnings of this world is found in **Hebrews 11:3: "By faith we understand that the universe was formed at God's command, so that what is seen was not made out of what was visible."**

Now, there's an explanation I can understand: simple, straightforward, and believable if you have a belief in a supreme being. Science says we cannot prove the existence of a supreme being, and therefore one does not exist. On the other hand, they cannot prove that the origin of the species is true, yet they expect us to believe it because they are intellectually superior and tell us so. Are we to believe God and his Word or are we to believe the lie?

Satan's objective is always to cast doubt on the truth of God's Word, and he loves to deal in obvious absolutes based upon the world's wisdom. I saw an example of this in a TV commercial. The commercial was for a medicine to relieve the symptoms of Chronic Obstructive Pulmonary Disease and at the end of the commercial it said, "Of course the effects of COPD cannot be reversed." The kingdom of the world expresses absolutes that have little or no hope and are always contrary to the great hope of the kingdom of God.

Make no mistake about it: when I'm speaking of the kingdom of God, I make absolute statements too, but they are based upon what God says and not human wisdom. I cannot fault the people of the kingdom of the world, for they can believe only what they believe in. I can, however, fault the residents of the kingdom of God for believing the lies of the kingdom of the world. I can see only two reasons for doing this. Either they are ignorant of the promises of the kingdom of God, or they, like their ancestors, are choosing to believe the lie rather than the truth.

The world says there is no permanent hope for the sufferers of COPD, but God's Word says in **Matthew 9:35, "Jesus went through all the towns and villages, teaching in their synagogues, preaching the good news of the kingdom and healing every disease and sickness."** Then we retort, "Yes, but that was Jesus." But then we look further to the Word of God, and it says in **James 5:14–15, "Is any one of you sick? He should call the elders of the church to pray over him and anoint him with oil in the name of the Lord. And the prayer offered in faith will make the sick person well; the Lord will raise him up."** Okay, now maybe we are without excuse.

I believe that if we were to have health, prosperity, and holiness, our lives would be complete. Literally, that's all it would take. By the same token, every area of our carnal life falls under one of the three headings: science, commerce, or religion. Occasionally I find something that I just can't figure out how to categorize. We recently went through a very contentious political campaign (aren't they all?). This got me to wondering which heading politics would fall under. As the campaign went on and the astronomical amount of money spent became headline news, the answer to my question became more and more obvious. Then I saw a tidbit that convinced me of the proper answer. It was reported that after he leaves office, a president of the United States will be worth more than $100 million when he dies. Politics is big business; it may even be the force that drives commerce.

Each of these three has but one purpose, and that is to subvert the way of God. If we consider both the Word of God and the way of the world, we will see that they are almost always diametrically opposed to each other. We are told in **1 Corinthians 3:19, "For the wisdom of this world is foolishness in God's sight"** and again in **1 Corinthians 2:18, "For the message of the cross is foolishness to those who are perishing."** The world is foolishness to God, and the very foundation of God's gift of salvation is foolishness to man. Can we not begin to see that there is a tug-of-war for the hearts of men and more so for man's belief system?

I recently saw a video of an eight-month-old baby who was born deaf. The baby was hooked up to some type of bio-feed through which he could hear his mother for the first time, and his reaction was precious. But as wonderful as that was, the moment they take the bio-feed off his head, he is again thrown into a world of absolute silence. It made my heart ache to think of how confused he would be. The world always costs. It seems to me that God rather enjoys giving people hearing, sight, and any other healing they need for free. I'm telling you, people, God wants us to be whole and healthy. All we need to do is trust him for it. Do not believe that the world can do that for you through science, commerce, or religion.

Each of the three areas has a specialty. Commerce is the most anti-man, as it preys on our lusts. Science is the most anti-God, as its whole purpose is to deny God and to create an environment in which God is not needed. Religion is the most anti-Jesus for its contends we can be holy because of what we do and not only because of what Jesus has done.

I am going to end this chapter with a simple question and my answer. What is your definition of the world? It would seem to me, considering God has said that friendship with the world makes you an enemy of God, that defining what the world is makes very good sense. So what is your definition of the world? Do not misunderstand me: I'm not going to throw the baby out with the bathwater. I like central heat and indoor plumbing. I have done without both but much prefer life with them and am very thankful to God that I have them. My answer is quite simple. Anything that disagrees to any extent with the simple Word of God or with anything that attempts to aid in the fulfillment of the simple promises of God is of the world. God said what he meant and doesn't need any help to fulfill his promises. Another way to tell whether something is of God or the world is remembering that the world causes angst and pain. God causes neither.

CHAPTER 14

Secrets

I have a question for you. What is the secret to life? The answer is somewhat of a riddle. For you see, the secret to life is death. Jesus says in **John 10:10, "I have come that they may have life, and have it to the full."** But the only way to receive this life is to die to self. **"For whoever wants to save his life will lose it" (Matthew 16:25).**

We touched upon this idea of death to self earlier in this book. However, it so ties into the concept of giving up the world that I think it would pay to look at it further. You see, I'm not convinced that I have convinced you that it is absolutely essential that we fully comprehend what God means when he says friendship with the world makes you his enemy.

If we are friends with the world, God does not love us any less. The problem is that we will love him less. "No servant can serve two masters: for either he will hate the one, and love the other; or else he will hold to the one, and despise the other. **Ye cannot serve God and mammon" (Luke 16:13 KJV).** I used the King James Version for that quote because it is faithful to the word *mammon*, whereas most other translations use the word *money*. Money is actually an incomplete thought in relation to the word *mammon*. *Mammon* actually refers to a god of covetousness. This is exactly what the world does to us. It makes us covet that which the world offers on the world's terms. **"For everything in the world—the cravings of sinful man, the lust of his eyes and the boasting of what he has and does—comes not from the Father but from the world" (1 John 2:16).** The world seduces us by giving us a thought, which becomes an obsession, and then we work to fulfill it. The ironic part is that whatever the world offers, God wants to freely give us something better.

"What good will it be for a man if he gains the whole world, yet forfeits his soul? Or what can a man give in exchange for his soul?" (Matthew 16:26). These are two questions that Jesus asks and that every person who has ever lived will answer. Most of the time, the answer will be through our actions. If we were asked point-blank whether we would rather have all of the world or eternal salvation for our souls, undoubtedly we would quickly answer that we choose our souls. But is Jesus actually asking us to make a choice between the world and our souls? And how much of the world do we gain before we lose our souls? Or is it a proportional thing, that is, to gain a little world, we are going to lose a little soul? Jesus' question is provocative, but do we ever really consider answering it? When Jesus asks us what we can give in exchange for our souls, the obvious answer is the whole world. Basically he is asking us the same question in two different ways. What's more important, the world or our souls? By asking the question, he is requiring us to make a choice.

"Then Jesus said to his disciples, 'If anyone would come after me, he must deny himself and take up his cross and follow me'" (Matthew 16:24). What is this cross we are to pick up except maybe the very denial that he speaks of? And what is it that we are to deny ourselves but the world? **"May I never boast except in the cross of our Lord Jesus Christ, through which the world has been crucified to me, and I to the world" (Galatians 6:14).** What are you when you are crucified? You are dead. So what does

Galatians 6:14 say except that the world should not be my life or even maybe in my life? It should be dead to me and me to it. **"Put to death, therefore, whatever belongs to your earthly nature"** **(Colossians 3:5).**

Paul said that he preached Christ and Christ crucified (1 Corinthians 2:2). If all we preach is a crucified Christ, we have nothing but a dead holy man, and that is not what Paul meant. We need to understand Christ crucified, but we need to live Christ resurrected. For you see, the crucifixion is victory over the world, but the resurrection is life in God. And just as truly as I died crucified in Christ, I have my life in the resurrected Christ, and that is where the promises reside. **"I have been crucified with Christ and I no longer live, but Christ lives in me" (Galatians 2:20). "In God's great mercy** *he has given us new birth* **into a living hope** *through the resurrection of Jesus Christ* **from the dead" (1 Peter 1:3, italics mine).**

What is this living hope we are given by the new birth through the resurrection? The answer is a life that is completely different from the one we knew before we were resurrected through the new birth. But just like everything, it must be received to be lived. It is a promise, but unless we acknowledge and receive the promise, it does not become reality. If someone gives me a check for $10,000, it is simply a promise of money. It does not become reality until I take it to the bank and cash it or deposit it. The promises of God are much the same. If we do not claim them, cash them—that is, take them as our own—they remain for us simply words on paper.

"Do not conform any longer to the pattern of this world, but be transformed by the renewing of your mind. Then you will be able to test and approve what God's will is—his good, pleasing and perfect will" (Romans 12:2). This is a very interesting Scripture and much more provocative than we would give it credit for. For instance, let's look at it backward. To find God's will, we must be able to test and approve our actions, but to do that, we must be transformed. But to have that happen, we must have a renewed mind, and for that to happen, we must no longer conform to the pattern of this world. Sounds simple, but most of us have never even considered what the pattern of this world is that we are no longer to be conformed to.

Over time I have asked several people about their definition of the world. Now remember, God says friendship with the world sets us apart from him. When I ask people this question, I invariably get a blank stare, usually followed by a lot of hemming and hawing. Never have I received a pre-thought-out answer. One would think that when God says we cannot love him and the world, we would spend some time earnestly—maybe even a little fearfully—considering what this horrible thing is that God tells us to have nothing to do with.

I have considered that question. Bear in mind that in the forefront of my consideration was the fact that I like indoor plumbing. I am not at all inclined to throw the baby out with the bathwater. I am a horseman, but when I go to town, I do not want to take the horse and buggy. I want to take my car, which has heat in the winter and air-conditioning in the summer, and I want to take it out of my heated garage. Braced with these dilemmas, I considered my answer carefully. Then I asked God what he thought. He said it is a spiritual question, and that therefore, I should find a spiritual answer. This is the answer I came up with: *anything on which we depend to aid or fulfill the promises of God is of the world.*

The Israelites found themselves in a similar situation. They were called out of the world with which they were familiar and where most of their needs were provided for, although under duress. God led them out of Egypt (remember we talked of Egypt before) into a place with which they were totally unfamiliar and where they needed to depend upon him totally on their way to the Promised Land. Once we have accepted new life through Jesus, we are in exactly the same place. We are called out of a world with which we are familiar and where our needs have been met, at least to some extent, into a new world of faith. Like the Israelites, we are called to two things. We are called to not look back or return to the previous world, and we are called to depend upon a faithful God to provide.

Have you ever read a Scripture many times and failed to see something in it or to read it wrong? I recently had that experience with a passage in Hebrews. Hebrews 3 is speaking of the Israelites' journey and the "time of testing in the desert." I always thought this testing was God testing the Israelites, but I recently read the passage and saw clearly that it was the Israelites testing God. In those days, they were provided food and water, their clothing never wore out, and when they asked for more, God gave it to them. Yet they did not trust him, and longed to return to the bondage of Egypt. For forty years they saw what God did, and yet they did not believe. **"That is why I was angry with that generation, and I said, 'Their hearts are always going astray, and they have not known my ways'" (Hebrews 3:10).** Because of unbelief, they were caught somewhere between the bondage of the past and the glory of the Promised Land. In this passage, God speaks of a rest they can enter only by believing. The people he led out of bondage could never enter this rest, because they would not let go of the past, nor would they completely trust God with their present or future. **"See to it, brothers, that none of you has a sinful, unbelieving heart that turns away from the living God" (Hebrews 3:12).** In this passage, the heart is not unbelieving because it is sinful; rather it is sinful because it is unbelieving. **"So we see that they were not able to enter, because of their unbelief" (Hebrews 3:19).**

"For you were once darkness, but now you are light in the Lord. Live as children of light (for the fruit of the light consists in all goodness, righteousness and truth) and find out what pleases the Lord" (Ephesians 5:8–10). We know from Hebrews 11:6 that without faith it is impossible to please God, so I do not think it is a stretch to say that faith pleases God. Faith is an eternal thing. It cannot exist in the temporal life we have been called out of, so let us go on and try to figure out how to leave behind the temporal Egypt and move into the faith ground of the kingdom of God.

CHAPTER 15

The Theist

You were taught, with regard to your former way of life, to put off your old self, which is being corrupted by its deceitful desires; to be made new in the attitude of your minds; and to put on the new self, created to be like God in true righteousness and holiness.
—Ephesians 4:22–24

God can be known only from the eternal. The flesh is of flesh and the spirit is of spirit. The flesh is temporal; the spirit is eternal.

The eternal God is spirit, and we can know him only in spirit.

Here are three things to help us move from the temporal to the eternal:

1) Knowing who I am.

We can know the I Am only when we know who we are. **"How great is the love the Father has lavished on us, that we should be called children of God! And that is what we are!"** **(1 John 3:1).**

Matthew 1:17 lists three separate lists of fourteen generations from Abraham to Christ, but the last group has only thirteen generations.

That is because we are the fourteenth generation of God. All who were born after Christ and have accepted their rebirth in Christ are the fourteenth generation of God.

"Christ lives in me" (Galatians 2:20). That is the exchanged life—exchanging our life for his. We can live his only after we give up ours. **"Put to death, therefore, whatever belongs to your earthly nature" (Colossians 3:5).** Second Corinthians 6:6 declares that we are the temple of the living God. Hebrews 7:21 calls us in Christ a priest forever according to the order of Melchizedek, and most exciting of all is 1 John 2:27, which says the anointing we received from Jesus remains in us. That is so exciting because the word used for anointing is *cristo,* which is the same word as *Christ.* The Scripture is very clearly saying that we have the same anointing as Jesus—that is, the same anointing that made him Christ is upon us.

So there we have it. Who am I? I am the fourteenth generation, I am he who Christ has made his own within, I'm a temple in which the living God dwells, I'm a priest of the most high, living God, and I have a sickness-rebuking, prosperity-giving, holiness-fulfilling anointing—the same as Jesus had.

It is summed up best by **1 Peter 2:9**, which says, **"We are a chosen people, a Royal priesthood, a holy nation, a people belonging to God."** The next line also takes us into number two: it says that we are called to be these things that we may declare the praises of him. We need to know that we are emperors, but even more, we need to know that we are emperors in borrowed clothes. The clothes that make us emperors are bought and paid for by Jesus the Christ.

2) Knowing why "I am."

We have already established that I am in Christ and Christ is in me. Therefore, it makes sense that what Christ was about, I should

119

be about. In fact, John said as much when he said, in 1 **John 2:6,** **"Whoever claims to live in him must walk as Jesus did."**

He died to self that others could live; I too am called to die to self. He was resurrected from death to free those who lived in bondage to death. I too am called to a resurrected life. **"We were therefore buried with him through baptism into death in order that, just as Christ was raised from the dead through the glory of the Father, we too may live a new life" (Romans 6:4).**

What was the greatest work that Christ did? I believe that John sums it up when he says Jesus came to destroy the works of the Devil. I believe this is also our greatest calling—to destroy the works of the Devil, to destroy them first in our own lives, then in the lives of our family, and then in the community around us. This is the warfare that we have been called to. **"For though we live in the world, we do not wage war as the world does. The weapons we fight with are not the weapons of the world. On the contrary, they have divine power to demolish strongholds. We demolish arguments and every pretension that sets itself up against the knowledge of God, and we take captive every thought to make it obedient to Christ" (2 Corinthians 10:3–5).**

3) Knowing how I am

The third thing that helps me move from the temporal to the eternal is knowing how I am to be successful. To be successful, one must examine one's priorities. Most of this warfare has to do with priorities. If my priorities are caught in the temporal, I will live and die in the temporal. That is why **1 John 2:15–17** is such a great warning:

> **Do not love the world or anything in the world. If anyone loves the world, the love of the Father is not in him. For everything in the**

world—the cravings of sinful man, the lust
of his eyes and the boasting of what he has
and does is not from the Father but from the
world. The world and its desires pass away,
but *the man who does the will of God lives forever.*
(1 John 2:15–17, italics mine)

To move from the temporal to the eternal, I must clearly move my
priorities from the world to the kingdom.

The book of Matthew tells us how to begin to make this move. **"But
seek first his kingdom and his righteousness" (Matthew 6:33).**

Matthew goes on to say that if our priorities are upon him first, then
the temporal things will be taken care of for us.

**"So do not worry, saying, 'What shall we eat?' or 'What shall
we drink?' or 'What shall we wear?' For the pagans run after
all these things, and your heavenly Father knows that you
need them. But seek first his kingdom and his righteousness,
and all these things will be given to you as well" (Matthew
6:31–33).**

Why is this so important? Because God is after our hearts, and a
very great truth is found in **Matthew 6:21**, which says, **"For where
your treasure is, there your heart will be also."** If our hearts
are caught in the world, they will produce that which is of the world:
greed and selfishness. It is not that God loves us less because we are
caught in the snare of the world; rather, we will love him less.

God is a God of love and calls us to be the same. It is one of the
great priorities. **"'He answered: "Love the Lord your God
with all your heart and with all your soul and with all your
strength and with all your mind"; and, "Love your neighbor**

as yourself." 'You have answered correctly,' Jesus replied. 'Do this and you will live'" (Luke 10:27–28). If we do this, not only will we live, but he will use us to be life givers. But there is a prerequisite to be able to do this. We cannot be full of God if we are full of self. If left to our own devices, we will always seek self first and those things that gratify self—the cravings of sinful man, the lust of his eyes, and the boasting of what he has and does. This filling up of self is exactly opposite of what the Father and the Son have done for us. **"The Father so loved the world that he gave his one and only Son, that whoever believes in him shall not perish but have eternal life" (John 3:16). "The Son being in very nature God, did not consider equality with God something to be grasped, but made himself nothing, taking the very nature of a servant, being made in human likeness. And being found in appearance as a man, he humbled himself and became obedient to death—even death on a cross!" (Philippians 2:6–8).** God is showing us examples of love and obedience that we may do the same.

The book of Jude gives us a clear pattern to move up from the temporal to the eternal. **"But you, dear friends, build yourselves up in your most holy faith and pray in the Holy Spirit" (Jude 1:20).** Doing spiritual things brings spiritual results.

"The life I live in the body, I live by faith in the Son of God" (Galatians 2:20). What is this faith life like? What is it like to claim God's promises as our own and to feel his intimate care of us? For me the best-written example of life in the promises of God is the Twenty-Third Psalm. I do not know why this is read at funerals, for it is the greatest piece of literature describing the results of God's promises in a life if one believes. The Twenty-Third Psalm is about 120 words long, yet in this short poem, the author is telling us of at least fourteen promises that he has experienced God fulfilling in his life.

1) Guidance
2) Supply
3) Abundance
4) Peace
5) Restoration
6) Righteousness
7) Courage
8) Protection
9) Divine presence
10) Honor
11) Health
12) Provision for others
13) Angelic protection
14) Eternal salvation

It is amazing, all the other things that follow when we allow him to guide us,. What we must always remember is that **"the kingdom of God is not a matter of eating and drinking, but of righteousness, peace and joy in the Holy Spirit" (Romans 14:17).** *In other words, it is a life lived outside the conventions of normal life.*

Let's talk about definitions for a minute.

An atheist is a person who does not believe in the existence of God.

An agnostic claims neither faith in nor disbelief in God. He says the existence of God cannot be proved or disproved, and therefore he does not know whether there is a God.

A deist is one who accepts the existence of a single creator on the basis of reason but rejects belief in a supernatural deity who interacts with humankind.

A theist believes in one God as creator of the universe, intervening in it and sustaining a personal relationship with his creatures on a regular basis.

Most of us likely fall somewhere between a deist and a theist. We can reasonably see by looking around us that there is a God: "all this just couldn't be an accident." However, it is difficult for us to believe that on a moment-to-moment basis, he walks with us, talks with us, and creates miracles for us. We find it very difficult to understand that *if we believe, he creates our destiny.*

The greatest enemies of a deist are the miracles of God, and the greatest miracle of God is the resurrection.

Thomas Jefferson was a deist—so much so that he was the original cut-and-paste expert. He created his own Bible by cutting out all of the miracles and pasting it back together. Needless to say, it did not make a lot of sense.

However, he did create a great Constitution, putting men with checks and balances in control of the destiny of the masses, and the masses in control of those men. Fortunately for us, most of the framers of our government were theists and trusted and invoked God to make it work.

Jefferson had one advantage over us: he knew the Word. He deliberated over it to find every miracle to eliminate from his Bible. If we do not know the promises (everyday miracles), how can we appropriate them as our own? Jesus died for the sins of the whole world, but only those who confess belief in that truth are forgiven. It is the same with the promises. Only as we confess belief in them and live that belief do they become active in our lives. The promises of God are everyday miracles. They are meant to be a way of life. They're meant to be understood as the actions of a completely theistic

God who truly cares for us and all of our needs on a daily basis. Our part is to accept that care and to trust in it as our provision.

I described the resurrection as the greatest of miracles, but in truth, it's more of a promise. Through the resurrection, he promises us that what he did and what he said is true. One of the greatest things he said is **"But I tell you the truth: It is for your good that I am going away. Unless I go away, the Counselor will not come to you; but if I go, I will send him to you." (John16:7).** The Father's purpose for sending the Holy Spirit into our lives is to create miracles every day if we believe and we ask.

The Father gives us the miracle of life, and not just life, but abundant life. "I have come that you may have life and have it abundantly." To live out this miracle of abundant life, we need to understand only three other miracles.

The miracle of holiness—**Hebrews 8:12: "For I will forgive their wickedness and will remember their sins no more."**

The miracle of prosperity—**Philippians 4:19: "And my God will meet all your needs according to his glorious riches in Christ Jesus."**

The miracle of health—**3 John 1:2: "Dear Friend, I pray that you may enjoy good health and that all may go well with you, even as your soul is getting along well."**

The next chapters are devoted to convincing you that along with salvation and baptism in the Holy Spirit, belief in holiness, prosperity, and health is all we need to live long and joy-filled lives. Together we will look at the many Scriptures for each, and we will also compare the promises with the world's counterfeits.

CHAPTER 16

Holiness

*"For I know the plans I have for you," declares the
Lord, "plans to prosper you and not to harm you,
plans to give you hope and a future."*
—Jeremiah 29:11

This Scripture was given to the Israelites as the Lord was preparing
to bring them out of exile in Babylon. They would have been in
exile for seventy years and were going into a land that they called
home and yet had never seen. It would be a trip full of dangers and
new, scary places. I think the situation is comparable to where he is
calling us in these last days. And the Scripture definitely is a promise
we will need if we walk in what I believe the Lord is proposing in
the next chapters.

Each of us has a legend about ourselves. Some of the parts of this
legend are positive and some are negative. Some parts of this legend
are true and some are not. Some parts of this legend are understood
in our conscious and some in our subconscious. But all parts of this
legend combine to define who we think we are and who we present
to the world. These legends are so strong within the natural man
that we often defend them without reason. Three of these golden
calves that we often use to define ourselves are our occupations, our
religions, and our health. How many times have we heard or been

involved in conversations that started out with "How have you been? How is the family?" followed by "What have you been up to? Still at the same job?" The point I am making is that like the world, we find our identity in the things of the world, and this should not be. When we do this, our prosperity is found through our work, our health is found in either things we do like eating right or through the medical community, and our holiness is found in what we do and say or where and when we go to church.

When our identity comes from the world, we are of the world. Our identity should be found in Christ and him alone. **Acts 17:25 says, "… because he himself gives all men life and breath and everything else."** He himself is our complete provision and not anything we or the world have provided. Why has he done this? **"God did this so that men would seek him and perhaps reach out for him and find him" (Acts 17:27).** His hope is that when we find him, we will realize that he cares for us as his children, which we truly are. In his care, all we need to do is believe, and all is provided.

Acts 17:28 says, "'For in him we live and move and have our being.'" It is only as we realize this "in him-ness" of our existence and receive it by faith that we find our true legend, and then life as life abundant begins. In the next chapters I'm going to give you a whole new perspective on the above-mentioned golden calves of our old legends. Relative to these old legends, I am going to ask you to join me in **Philippians 3:13–14**, which says, **"Forgetting what is behind and straining toward what is ahead, we press on toward the goal to win the prize for which God has called us heavenward in Christ Jesus."** Together we will find our true identity and a new way of life creating our legend in him.

In these chapters, I will discuss holiness, prosperity, and health, sometimes comparing them with the Devil's counterfeits of religion, commerce, and science. These chapters are actually the purpose of this book; it has just taken me a lot of words to get here. So without further ado, let us consider holiness.

Holiness that is the holy character of God is the hardest of the three to explain. Paramount among these difficulties in understanding it for me was understanding the difference between being saved by faith, being sanctified by faith, and then allowing God to work out this sanctification by faith. I kept tripping over Scriptures using words like *salvation, sanctification, justification,* and *righteousness.* But then I came to the conclusion that the words weren't confusing me as much as my own religious paradigms were. It was in my mind that if I was to look up a passage on salvation, it would be talking about holiness, but I did not always find that to be the case. Many times these words in scriptural context did not convey the meaning I meant. Suddenly, it was as if a light was turned on, and I saw that we were talking about three different things.

Salvation is just that. When we are saved, we are going to heaven by faith in Jesus Christ and his atonement for our sins. However, that does not guarantee us heaven on earth. Living out heaven on earth is a whole different work of the Holy Spirit.

> **For no one can lay any foundation other than the one already laid, which is Jesus Christ. If any man builds on this foundation using gold, silver, costly stones, wood, hay or straw, his work will be shown for what it is, because the Day will bring it to light. It will be revealed with fire, and the fire will test the quality of each man's work. If what he has built survives, he will receive his reward. If it is burned up, he will suffer loss; he himself will be saved,**

**but only as one escaping through the flames.
(1 Corinthians 3:11–15)**

This Scripture has gone a long way toward making me understand the process. Jesus Christ is the foundation, and we discovered how we accept him and become saved in earlier chapters. But the foundation is only the base. It is what and how we build upon this base that holiness and righteousness is all about.

In the Scripture above, the building materials of gold, silver, and costly stones are materials of the kingdom; the wood, hay, and straw are materials of the world. Do not forget the harsh words God has to say about the world. If we are living as the world lives, we will be using the Devil's materials to construct our characters. If we have accepted the Holy Spirit's sanctification in our lives, we will be using heavenly materials to construct godly characters. Do not misunderstand: I do not mean we work this out; rather, I mean we allow the Holy Spirit to construct this within us. We must be sanctified (set apart) because we cannot be in the world and in Christ. It does not, however, mean that because we are saved, we are sanctified.

Hebrews 12:14 says, "Make every effort to live in peace with all men and to be holy; without holiness no one will see the Lord."

The purpose of this book is to show that the fulfillment of God's promises in our lives is entirely his doing and that all that is required of us is faith. However, the above Scripture seems to contradict that premise. The Scripture talks of *our effort* to live in peace and to be holy. Some years ago, if I found what seemed like a contradiction between what I thought was truth and a translation in the Word of God, I simply ignored it. There was this thing in me that would not allow the contemplation of a mistake in translation in the Word of

God. I would not consider a personal prejudice, a religious prejudice, or human error on the part of the translator, nor would I consider a misunderstanding on my part. Then several years ago I heard a teaching that became a permanent part of my theology. The form of worship I am involved in does not have a monologue as a sermon; rather it is a participatory dialogue in which all present can have an opportunity to speak. One Sunday one of the men in the group asked a question. Unfortunately, I can't share the exact phrase with you because my editor believes it has an innuendo of profanity, which violates their editorial practices. The question asked was whether it would be a good thing if I had a (four-word phrase that I cannot use). Initially, this was met with shock; most of us were just speechless. One other person in the group answered the question with a very positive yes. He said that for those of us who heat our homes with wood, it would be a very good thing, but that his way of expressing it was wrong by several hundred years. He went on to explain that the proper way to convey the message in today's society would be for the man to say he had a "large bundle of sticks on his donkey." Both sayings have the very same meaning; however, in our society, the first way of expressing it has come to be very offensive. The first individual's purpose was not to shock or offend us but rather to show us that although words may stay the same, how we interpret them can change. The above Scripture is a perfect example of this lesson.

I actually like the King James Version of this Scripture: **"Follow peace with all men, and holiness, without which no man shall see the Lord" (Hebrews 12:14 KJV).** I think I like this Scripture better than the NIV because it has about 32 percent fewer words. I am being somewhat of a hypocrite when I say this because of the many words I have used in this book to explain a very simple concept. However, when it comes to words, less is more. Words can unite and simplify, but mostly they confuse and divide. We have the Tower of Babel as an example of this. My premise in this whole thesis is that God provides all we need, and all we need to do is believe. The above Scripture, however, seems to contradict that point of view. I believe that Scripture is a perfect example of what I was talking about when I said that although words may stay the same, our interpretation of them changes.

The Scripture basically says we are to be holy. Does that not imply that we are to be without sin? According to *Webster's New World Dictionary of the American Language Collegiate Edition* the second-most popular definition of *holy* is "spiritually perfect or pure; untainted by evil or sin; sinless; saintly." I also believe this is what most of us think a holy man or woman is. In 1611, when the King James Bible was published, *holy* had a much simpler meaning. It meant "sanctified," which simply meant "set apart." Do you see what I mean about words changing? If we look at that Scripture with the definition of *holy* relating to our acts, it completely destroys my contention that all is by faith. However, if we understand that the word means—that we are set apart—it greatly substantiates my thoughts.

If I were to paraphrase this Scripture, it would say, "Follow peace with all men and accept being set apart from the world, for without peace and separation from the world, no one shall see the Lord." This holiness, this separation from the world, is not something we do; it is something we receive from the Lord. All we need to do is believe to receive.

Romans 5:8 says, **"But God demonstrates his own love for us in this: While we were still sinners, Christ died for us."** This is salvation in a nutshell: God's love and Christ's death.

First John 2:2 says, **"He is the atoning sacrifice for our sins, and not only for ours but also for the sins of the whole world."** We see from this Scripture that Jesus died not only for your sins but for the sins of the whole world. Does that mean everyone is going to heaven? Of course not. Then why are you? You are going to heaven because something was stirred inside you to see the truth and to receive it by faith. I contend that sanctification and justification/ righteousness are received in exactly the same way. They are not any more automatic than forgiveness for our sins. We must receive them by faith.

Colossians 1:21–22 says, **"Once you were alienated from God and were enemies in your minds because of your evil behavior. But now he has reconciled you by Christ's physical body through death to present you holy in his sight, without blemish and free from accusation."** What a magnificent scriptural promise! He took us who showed him contempt and reached out through his son to make us acceptable to be called his loved ones. But unless we receive this holiness (set-aside-ness) by faith, it has no life-changing value for us, just as salvation was of no value until we received it by faith.

For years I have heard Christians refer to themselves as old sinners saved by grace. I accepted that theology until the Lord showed me what sanctification was all about. Now I tell people I am a saint who might occasionally sin. Why do I do that? Because I don't want to disagree with my heavenly Father. Every time I refer to myself as a sinner, I am accusing myself. The Scripture above says I am free of accusation. Why would I disagree with God? I want to see me as God sees me: holy and without blemish. But I can do it only through faith in what he has declared finished. Why would he do this for me? In a word, it is called grace. *Grace* defined is "unmerited favor." I do not want to go into the topic of grace, as I do not have the space to do it justice. I do recommend three books on grace, because it is absolutely imperative that we understand the wonder of grace if we are to prosper on this side of heaven in the kingdom of God. The first book is by Joseph Prince and called *Destined to Reign*. The second book is by Philip Yancey and is called *What's So Amazing About Grace?* The third book is *The Grace Awakening* by Charles Swindoll.

Isn't Christianity wonderful? Here I am, going to heaven when I die as pure as the driven snow, and I haven't done anything. Okay, I believed, but that was it. What a deal! Kind of like going to the car dealership to buy a new car and having them give it to you and throw in lifetime maintenance plus gas. This is like holiness works. Once you receive it by faith, God sees you as pure as his Son, Jesus. That sort of forbearance can only be driven by love and defined by grace.

There is a problem, however, and that is with me. When I get angry, I do not feel holy. When I get jealous, I do not feel holy. When lust rises up in me, I do not feel holy. The list of times I do not feel holy can go on and on. These things do not make God see me as any less holy, but they certainly affect me and those around me. **"I do not understand what I do. For what I want to do I do not do, but what I hate I do" (Romans 7:15).** This is a dilemma.

Have you ever noticed that God is the God of the dilemma? I do not mean to say that he causes the dilemma; rather, he uses the dilemma to provoke us into a better place. My wife and I have seen this countless times, both in our ministering to others and in our personal lives. Everything will be going along fine and then suddenly we encounter a situation that we can find no way around. Sometimes we know what we are supposed to do but it's just too hard, and sometimes we're just confused. Let me give you an example. I have a friend who had a debt he thought had been taken care of. He found out not only that he still owed the money, but that great pressure was being applied to pay it immediately. He came to me, and I asked him simply what God was saying to him. He replied that he just needed more trust. This did not sound right to me, but I couldn't put my finger on exactly what was happening. As I considered it quietly that evening, it suddenly came to me what the problem was. It was not that this gentleman needed to trust more; it was that he needed to fear less. As soon as pressure came, his tendency was to fear. When I communicated this to him, he immediately had a light go on and repented of his fear. He then negotiated the crisis from a God position and it was over almost immediately.

As you can see, from a God perspective, the situation was not about money at all but rather about my friend's trip through life. No longer was he to be dominated by fear but rather by victory. And that is precisely what God is all about: delivering us from ourselves so that we can live a victorious kingdom life.

Something my wife and I say to each other almost daily is "We live such a blessed life." In fact, whenever a problem or dilemma raises its head in our life and interferes with our blessedness, we immediately ask God what he is wanting to put into our life and what we should be taking out. If you remember, I talked of being confused about salvation, sanctification, and justification/righteousness, and it wasn't until I divided them into three segments that I began to understand. We spoke of salvation as just that by faith. We spoke of sanctification as accepting by faith our separation from the world. Justification/righteousness comes after sanctification and is a process by which God leads us down certain roads. By faith we accept that leading and follow the road, thereby learning his Lordship over our lives and developing his character as ours. This is what I will refer to as the responsibility of kingdom living, literally death to the old man.

Romans 9:21 says, **"Does not the potter have the right to make out of the same lump of clay some pottery for noble purposes and some for common use?"** This is somewhat of an obscure Scripture, but I like it for many different purposes. Now I think it somewhat describes me and my mission with this book. I believe the Lord has given me a purpose in writing this book, to let you know the beneficial side of kingdom living. But that is the less noble side of the kingdom's purposes. A much more noble side of the kingdom is our necessity to die to the old man and his ways so that we are messengers of peace, love, and kingdom principles. In other words we are Jesus Christ to a dying world. That is what I referred to as the sacrificial side of kingdom living. However, if you want to read about that side of the kingdom of God, there are many good books out there. One I highly recommend is *The Myth of a Christian Religion* by Gregory A. Boyd. Now that I have expressed that genuine disclaimer, I will return to the less noble work the potter has destined me for. That is telling you the goodness of the kingdom he wants to pour out upon you, although I must warn you that the next part of this book leans heavily toward the sacrificial side of the kingdom. There is much benefit to justification/righteousness, but it does call us to and is the very essence of sacrifice.

The third part of this trilogy is justification/righteousness. As the two words mean practically the same thing, I will use *righteousness* from now on. *Righteousness* used to be pronounced right-wise-ness, which accurately describes the meaning. Righteousness is the process by which our heavenly Father teaches us the right and wise way to make kingdom decisions in our lives. It is the process through which he takes us to leave behind the world and walk deeper into kingdom living. One could possibly describe it as walking-out sanctification. But as I call it a process and describe it as walking out, do not misunderstand me: it is entirely by faith. **"Even the righteousness of God which is by faith of Jesus Christ unto all and upon all them that believe" (Romans 3:22).** Perhaps one could refer to it as faith unto obedience. I will endeavor to explain this phenomenon of righteousness in two different ways. One is scriptural and the other is experiential.

If we are talking faith, we are not going to get far down that road before we run into what seems like two different philosophies. On one hand we have James, who says faith without works is dead, and on the other hand we have Paul, who says faith and faith alone is sufficient. I personally do not believe that one ideology excludes the other. Both men agree that works of the law are of no value. So what are they talking about? Maybe if we look at this, it can help us in our understanding of righteousness.

When he mentions Abraham's righteousness in Romans 4, Paul says Abraham believed God and it was credited to him as righteousness. This refers to an incident in Genesis 15. James, when he speaks of Abraham's righteousness, is speaking about an incident in Genesis 22. In Genesis 15, Abraham was declared righteous because he believed God. However, he was not proved righteous until the twenty-second chapter. This proving—or as James called it, works—is what gives life to our righteousness.

In chapter 22, God says he is testing (proving) Abraham by having him offer his only son as a burnt offering. When it becomes obvious that Abraham is going to do as God asked, God stops him. Then God reiterates the promises he formerly gave to Abraham because, in God's words, "Abraham obeyed him." By faith God calls to us, and by faith we obey the calling. This obeying is called righteousness and refers to the works of which James is speaking. If we do not obey does that mean we are unrighteous, no, it simply means we will miss out on something good that Father God has for us.

This is not about obeying a set of rules or a general command; it is obeying something that God speaks to us specifically. I say this because in Genesis 17, God orders Abraham to circumcise every man in his household. This is a general command, and Abraham obeys. Now, it would seem to me that if I was over eighty years old and God told me to get circumcised and I obeyed, that would be a big proof of my obedience. However, it is not credited to Abraham as righteousness. Only obeying the specific call to sacrifice the son he loved fulfilled righteousness. It is the same way today. Only when God speaks specific things to us and we obey is his righteousness fulfilled within us.

This story of Abraham has a lot more going on than we see on the surface. Abraham like all of us resembles an iceberg: 10 percent is visible, 90 percent is below the surface. The story of Abraham gives us some hints about what God was doing. Isaac is referred to as the one Abraham loved and also as his only son. At this time Abraham had at least one more son, Ishmael. Remember the story I told a few minutes ago about the man who had financial problems but really had fear problems? When he was delivered of his fear, the financial problems disappeared. Maybe Abraham had some kind of over-the-top attachment to things of the world that exhibited itself through his relationship with Isaac. Maybe this attachment prevented a closer, more trusting relationship with his heavenly Father. I would contend that a portion of Abraham's carnality was left on the mountain, replaced by an equal proportion of spirituality. The old man went up the mountain, and part of him came down the new man. This is exactly what righteousness is all about: the ongoing process of allowing God to create the new man in his time and his way. We just have to believe to receive.

There was another way that God used to show me salvation, sanctification, and justification/righteousness. Some time ago as I was struggling through the definitions of each term and how they are different from but depend on one another, I was shown a simple visual. Salvation opens the door to the kingdom of God, but our backs are to the door and we are still facing the world. When we receive, by faith, sanctification, we turn around, and now our backs are to the world and we are looking into the kingdom of God. What we see is a path leading into the kingdom, and we may even be able to see the celestial city far in the distance. This path is what we would call justification/righteousness. As we step into the kingdom and proceed down the path, we will come to junctions. At each of these junctions, we will be presented with a choice. We will be asked to sacrifice some human Isaac in order to receive a divine promise. Sometimes because we don't understand, because we are afraid, or maybe we just can't, we do not sacrifice the Isaac. When this happens, we proceed down the wrong path. We are still headed toward the celestial city, but the path we are now on is no longer straight and narrow. It has deep valleys and steep hills and is full of dark and scary places. All of us have worldly strongholds within us, and only as we are willing to give them up do we develop kingdom strongholds. This is a lifelong process of developing righteousness, that is, the ability to make right—wise—kingdom decisions. All we need to do is by faith, know that when God calls us to release something, it is for something better.

I have a saying: "Every time I have been delivered of something in my life, it has been instantaneous, after about twenty years of struggle." The deliverance is God; the struggle is me. I believe as this process has gone on within me, I have cut the time down by at least a couple of years.

"For therein is the righteousness of God revealed from faith to faith: as it is written, The just shall live by faith" (Romans 1:17 KJV).

The above Scripture describes this lifelong process. As we receive a healing or deliverance from some worldly attribute by faith, it increases our faith and frees us to believe for more. We find holiness only in Jesus Christ through kingdom faith.

CHAPTER 17

Blocking the Benefits

But you were washed, you were sanctified, you were justified in the name of the Lord Jesus Christ and by the Spirit of our God.

—1 Corinthians 6:11

Washed, sanctified, and justified: the triune experience. Abraham had a similar triune experience. In Genesis 14 he hears God, in Genesis 17 he believes God, and in chapter 22 he obeys God. This is exactly what we are speaking about when we talk about the gift called holiness. We are first called, and then as we believe the calling, we are freed to obey.

And I do not mean obey the rules; I did not mean that we are to be Pharisees and believe highly of ourselves because we do do this and we don't do that. What I mean by obedience is that when the Spirit of God speaks to us about something in our lives that does not glorify the godliness within us, we obediently sacrifice it on the altar of Isaac. These habits and things we so desperately hang on to cause us and those around us nothing but anxiety and pain. That is precisely why the Father wants to remove them from our lives.

Salvation, sanctification, and righteousness all work together in this phenomenon that I am calling holiness. All are by faith, and all require some degree of obedience, but mostly they require us to give up our paradigms and prejudices. As we open our minds to the possibilities, we will begin to see the many benefits afforded to us when we embrace by faith this gift of holiness.

Some benefits of holiness are (1) a true knowledge of your specialness as a child of God; (2) victory over sin because you know it no longer testifies to who you are, so it loses its power in your life; (3) victory over fear, for you are much more aware of his care for you; (4) victory over the lust of the eyes, the lust of the flesh, and the boastful pride of life; (5) because of the above victories, the world has no more control of your life; (6) most important of all, it leaves no room for self-righteousness, because we receive holiness only when we realize he has done it all. It is called grace—unbelievable, wonderful, fulfilling grace.

I do not mean to imply by the meager list above that it includes all the benefits of holiness. I believe the list could be almost limitless. But not withstanding its strength in numbers, it remains somewhat fragile. As the title of this chapter implies, although holiness is a gift from God received by faith and therefore not subject to recall, the benefits of holiness can be muted. It may be a little surprising to you, but I consider religion the number one killer of the benefits of holiness.

The religion I am talking about as defined by *Webster's New Collegiate Dictionary* is "a personal set or institutionalized system of religious attitudes, beliefs, and practices." This set or system becomes a laundry list of do's and don'ts and quickly degenerates into man's worthless effort to please God. Society benefits greatly from man's attention to morals, but it is not what attracts God to us. In fact, it hinders, because not far down the road of my good morals, I begin to become self-righteous. If I were given only one word to describe religiosity, it would have to be *self-righteous*. Oh, wait: maybe that's two words. Oh well, you get my point.

The greatest biblical example of religious self-righteousness is the Pharisees. Jesus had a difficult time dealing with the Pharisees, and it is no less true today when one must deal with present-day Pharisees (which I don't). The biggest weapon of the religious is judgment and always their standard and biblical interpretation of what's right and what's wrong. The twin of judgment is gossip, which sometimes leads to slander. Judgment/gossip is the pillory of the modern church. Above all, God calls his kingdom people to love and peace, both of which are hard to maintain under the probing eye of judgment/gossip. Of course, the underlying power of judgment/gossip is our corporate interpretation of what sin is and what it is not.

In religion, sin is the enemy of holiness. In the kingdom, holiness has nothing to do with sin. Let me explain. Holiness has everything to do with faith and grace. But in the religion of the world, sin and works are the tools we use to measure someone's holiness. Lots of good works and they are holy; a little sin, and they are not. If the church was to understand holiness correctly, it would have to completely reinvent itself, and possibly it could not even survive. If holiness was understood to be a gift from God (grace) that has nothing to do with any of our actions except belief, the power to control people would be greatly diminished. In a nutshell, the general teaching of the church is that if you are a sinner, you need us so we can help you become holy, and if you are currently holy, you need us to stay that way. These positions can easily be defended by the Word, but do they truly represent God's positions on sin and holiness?

There will be those who say I am easy on sin. I certainly hope so, for as I look at the life of my Lord, he seemed pretty easy on sin. Remember the woman caught in adultery. It seems to me the only time he came down hard on people was when it came to the Pharisees and how they judged others compared with themselves. You see, in this sense holiness is the great equalizer. In the kingdom of God, we all receive it the same way—by faith, irrespective of our actions. Honestly, I cannot brag about my holiness, nor can I detract from anyone else's, for it is God's gift to us and is without recall.

Let us consider for a moment God's view of sin and the law. **"[T]hrough Christ Jesus the law of the Spirit of life set me free from the law of sin and death" (Romans 8:2).** Okay, according to this Scripture, I have been set free from the law of sin. **"God made him who had no sin to be sin for us, so that in him we might become the righteousness of God" (2 Corinthians 5:21).** Jesus became my sin. **Colossians 1:13–14 says, "… the Son he loves, in whom we have redemption, the forgiveness of sins."** Jesus forgives my sin. **Second Corinthians 5:19** says, **"God was reconciling the world to himself in Christ, not counting people's sins against them."** And he says my sins don't count. Sounds pretty soft on sin.

I fully realize there are many Scriptures that tell us to stop sinning, but these prohibitions have nothing to do with God's relationship with us. His love and covenant relationship with us is a constant, not subject to our actions but rather only his commitments to us. The reasons for any prohibitions against sin are summed up in Romans 13, among other places. **"The commandments, 'Do not commit adultery,' 'Do not murder,' 'Do not steal,' 'Do not covet,' and whatever other commandment there may be, are summed up in this one rule: 'Love your neighbor as yourself.' Love does no harm to its neighbor. Therefore love is the fulfillment of the law" (Romans 13:9–10).** You see, our determination to do what is right and not sin should come from our commitment to our neighbors, not to God. And yet when we consider our holiness in relationship to our actions, we are in grave danger of actually blocking the effect of holiness in our own life. Not far down the road of this self-righteousness we will find ourselves comparing our faux righteousness to our neighbors' lack, and in that, there is no love, and the law may no longer be fulfilled.

Whereas our love is very much dependent upon people's actions, God's love is not, and it cannot depend upon our actions except our action of belief. God is love. Therefore, God's love cannot be measured any more than God can be measured, nor does it have shadow. Once we express our acceptance of his love as completely summed up in the sacrifice of his Son, it is a constant to us, because he is a constant. It represents the same concept that because God is eternal, in him there is no time. Understanding this constant of God's love is important to our acceptance of holiness. It takes the effort of our always trying to earn God's love out of the equation. **Ephesians 3:17–19** says, **"And I pray that you, being rooted and established in love, may have power, together with all the saints, to grasp how wide and long and high and deep is the love of Christ, and to know this love that surpasses knowledge—that you may be filled to the measure of all the fullness of God."** *That you may be filled to the measure of all the fullness of God* pretty well describes holiness and can be fully appreciated only as you know God loves you no matter what (that is grace, or unmerited favor).

The church is a co-conspirator with this blocking of the benefits. I am not going to spend a lot of time, ink, or effort condemning or even considering the church. There are plenty of good books dedicated to pointing out the error of our ways. Notably, among them are several of the published works of Charles Newbold, Gregory Boyd, and *Houses That Change the World* by Wolfgang Simpson. With that said, I will discuss two facets of the church that I believe directly affect our understanding and acceptance of holiness.

The church seems somewhat confused about who or what it is. I would refer to a section of a book that some people refer to as the second Protestant Bible: <u>*Systematic Theology,*</u> Wayne Grudem (Inter-Varsity Press, Leicester, Great Britain and Zondervan Publishing

143

House, Grand Rapids, Michigan 1994) a volume one must respect for its girth if nothing else. I refer to page 866, part b, section 2 of Chapter 44, called "True and False Churches Today." In this section he implies that if the preaching in a congregation is pure preaching of the Word, and the gospel message of salvation by faith in Christ alone is preached, it is a true church, and the inference would be it is not a false church. This sort of thinking gives the church a top-down model, which is simply incorrect. The pastor does not establish whether a congregation is true or false; the hearts of the believers establish that. In defense of *Systematic Theology* I somewhat agree with Chapter 44 part C "The Purposes of the Church."

This organizational type we generally refer to as church in itself hinders our acceptance of holiness. The top-down model is very much like the corporate model of the workplace. One difference is that the church refers to its leaders as servants, but much of the time we find them to be overlords. Little room is left for the prophetic word if it does not come from the clericalist elite. This kind of sectarianism does not lend itself well to the proposition that all Christians are equal. The system of overlording does not lead us to an understanding that we are as loved and as anointed as any other member of the body of Christ. And this concept is crucial to our understanding of holiness. Holiness is the great equalizer, and clericalist thinking makes us Pharisees. When I try to explain a church with no organizational leadership to most people, they tell me it is not possible. I have, however, belonged to such a church for about fifteen years.

Jesus seemed to have no time for this overlord organizational system and in fact called his people to a mental overthrow of it—even to having been crucified outside the walls. He seemed to stress the acceptance and equality of all believers to the point of disobeying the rules so he could serve their needs.

Another problem the church has is its attitude that it is the moral compass for the world. It is not its job to point out the shortcomings of others; rather its job is to reconcile the world to the kingdom. **"All this is from God, who reconciled us to himself through Christ and gave us the ministry of reconciliation: that God was reconciling the world to himself in Christ, not counting men's sins against them. And he has committed to us the message of reconciliation" (2 Corinthians 5:18–19).**

The church has an obsession with sin and its need to keep itself pure, and yet this very occupation is what keeps it from being effective in the world. I'm going to tell you something quite shocking right now: my sin does not count. The Scripture above says God does not count my sin against me. A focus on sin keeps people caught in the grip of sin; that is the message of the seventh chapter of Romans. But the eighth chapter tells us of freedom. We need not focus on the old man and his ways, but as we focus on the new man and his holiness, we allow the Holy Spirit to remove from our lives the stains of sin. In the fellowship I belong to, we have the saying, *"If I have sin in my life, the problem is I do not have enough of the Holy Spirit."*

Before we go any farther, I must tell you I am not antinomian. I have read the first epistle of John, and I can assure you I have sinned and will probably sin again in the future. But our definitions of sin might differ. My definition of sin is anything I do that is not led by the Holy Spirit and does not benefit my neighbor. And please consider that my nearest neighbor is myself. I also do not believe that grace and the law/sin have anything to do with each other. Law and sin are of the world, and grace is of the kingdom. I may be in the world, but I am of the kingdom. **"For I died, and my life is now hidden with Christ in God" Colossians 3:3).** Therefore, what does not exist in the kingdom cannot exist in me. I may have symptoms because I am in the world and the Devil lies, but they are not real; I cannot have them, because they do not exist in the kingdom. This is a theme you will hear throughout the rest of this book. I recognize the symptoms are lies of the Devil, and as I resist him, he must flee. **"Submit yourselves, then, to God. Resist the devil, and he will flee from you"** (James 4:7).

"We know that anyone born of God does not continue to sin; the one who was born of God keeps him safe, and the evil one cannot harm him" (1 John 5:18). But if I do happen to sin, I know that **"If I confess my sins, he is faithful and just and will forgive me my sins and purify me from all unrighteousness" (1 John 1:9)** because of his promise to me that he has made me holy.

Condemnation is another huge holiness benefit blocker. Condemnation keeps us living in the past and under the bondage of sin. No matter how recent or how distant the past may be, it is still the past. We are instructed by **Philippians 1:13–14**, which says, **"But one thing I do: Forgetting what is behind and straining toward what is ahead, I press on toward the goal to win the prize for which God has called me heavenward in Christ Jesus."** Also the Word is very clear that condemnation should no longer have a place in our lives. **"Therefore, there is now no condemnation for those who are in Christ Jesus" (Romans 8:1).**

But the greatest holiness benefit blocker is simply our unbelief in the all-forgiving love of God.

This holiness that I speak of is God's promise that we receive by believing. Through this we receive a great number of advantages, the greatest of which is an overcoming, victorious life. **"The words 'it was credited to him' were written not for him alone, but also for us, to whom God will credit righteousness—for us who believe in him who raised Jesus our Lord from the dead. He was delivered over to death for our sins and was raised to**

life for our justification" (Romans 4:23–25). He was raised to life so that we are justified, but even more than that, when he came to life, so did we. **"And if the Spirit of him who raised Jesus from the dead is living in you, he who raised Christ from the dead will also give life to your mortal bodies through his Spirit, who lives in you" (Romans 8:11).**

CHAPTER 18

Prosperity

Whoever trusts in his riches will fall, but the righteous will thrive like a green leaf.

—Proverbs 11:28

Now listen, you rich people, weep and wail because of the misery that is coming upon you.

—James 5:1

People who want to get rich fall into temptation and a trap and into many foolish and harmful desires that plunge men into ruin and destruction. For the love of money is a root of all kinds of evil. Some people, eager for money, have wandered from the faith and pierced themselves with many griefs.

—1 Timothy 6:9–10

These may seem like strange Scriptures with which to begin a chapter on prosperity, but I thought it might be best to begin by telling you what this chapter is not about. I'm not sure that any of us except those who like to argue for the sake of argument would disagree that it is nicer to be rich than it is to be poor. However, as we look at the Scriptures above, we can see there are some serious inherent problems with being rich, and preachers who preach about prosperity for the purpose of our gaining riches are simply appealing to man's baser nature for their own gain.

I have absolutely no time or patience for those preachers who want to sell you some snake oil charm, guaranteeing you health or riches or whatever and calling it faith. They stand up in front of us with their smooth words, quoting Scripture; wearing expensive suits; flashing gold rings, expensive watches, and toothy smiles; and promising all the things of the world. They prey on people's needs and desires.

I was standing in the presence of such a preacher years ago as he bragged how he had put someone in their place. According to his story, a man approached him and told him of his need and asked for fifty dollars. The preacher said he told him in no uncertain words to get the money just like he had: by faith. Many thoughts went through my head at that moment, none of them complimentary to the preacher. However, I said nothing. The worst is that for a long time, I felt guilty for saying nothing, because to me the preacher's error was so obvious and the Word is so plain about giving to someone who asks (Matthew 5:42, Luke 6:30) that he should have been rebuked. One day as the Devil was peddling his guilt, I happened to see **Proverbs 9:7–8, "Whoever corrects a mocker invites insult; whoever rebukes a wicked man incurs abuse. Do not rebuke a mocker or he will hate you."** Suddenly, I realized that had I rebuked the preacher, I would have been reviled for my lack of faith not only by the preacher but by the other men standing by who believed like the preacher. Someone asked me if maybe I wasn't judging the many by the actions of one, and I said no, I thought I was judging the one by the actions of the many.

This chapter is also not about a magic percentage, a special prayer, or any other secret to getting rich through the good news of Jesus Christ.

Do you know what it takes to be prosperous in the kingdom of God? It takes just one thing. Faith is the only thing it takes. That's what this chapter is all about. I want to show you that God does want to bless his people with prosperity. No magic percentages, no special prayers, no secret rituals, just faith in a loving God and his desire for his people to be happy.

I personally have found that if I can find a Scripture to hang my hat on concerning a promise of God, I can believe. For me in relation to prosperity that Scripture is **2 Corinthians 8:9: "For you know the grace of our Lord Jesus Christ, that though he was rich, yet for your sakes he became poor, so that you through his poverty might become rich."**

Whenever I use this Scripture in reference to prosperity, invariably someone will say that's not what that Scripture means. Well, I'm here to tell you it certainly is! It means a whole lot of things, but one of its guarantees is our personal heavenly prosperity on earth. We often fail to consider the segmentation of the visitation of Jesus Christ to earth. By his very coming, we are guaranteed earthly possessions, a prosperous soul, and a rich relationship with our heavenly Father, just as we are guaranteed healing by the beating he took and remission of sins by the cross he hung upon. There is so much more, such as his death tearing the curtain of separation between us and our heavenly Father forever and his blood poured out on the ground at the foot of the cross and releasing the whole earth from the curse of original sin. But make no mistake about it, his arrival upon earth destroyed poverty forever. I do not know the financial condition of Joseph and Mary when they arrived in Bethlehem, but when they departed, they carried with them a baby boy and much bounty from the treasury of the kings of the East.

The history of God and man clearly shows God's intent to bless his people. Adam and Eve were created in a paradise where all of their needs were met. In Genesis 13 Abram is described as very wealthy in livestock and silver and gold. Both Jacob and Esau were very rich men. God's men were always well taken care of. Sure, there was some adversity in their lives, but mostly there was prosperity. David, for instance, was rich, and Solomon was wealthy beyond imagination. In the New Testament, Joseph and Mary left Bethlehem well supplied for their sojourn in Egypt, having been gifted gold, frankincense, and myrrh. Jesus himself had a treasury big enough to steal from, and when he died, his goods were enough to argue over, especially his cloak.

Any promise of God can be misused and can turn out to be a curse to us if we are not obedient. But none has greater potential for calamity than prosperity. It would seem there is a great deal of diversity concerning prosperity among the people who call upon God. On the one hand, there are those who will try anything and believe anybody to have the world's riches, and on the other hand, there are those who believe you cannot be a Christian and be prosperous. Both are dangerous and equally wrong. God intends for us to have things that make us comfortable. However, he knows the corrupting influence the things of the world have on his people.

"For the love of money is a root of all kinds of evil" (1 Timothy 6:10). You will notice God did not declare money evil; rather the lust for money can be a root out of which a bush of evil can grow in our lives. Actually, there is a parable in Luke 16 that I believe addresses both of these issues. In this parable a rich man has a manager who is squandering the wealth. The rich man calls for the manager to make an accounting so he can be dismissed from his position. The manager comes up with a scheme to cheat the rich man. There are many things to learn from this parable. Chief among them is that the rich man is God, and you will notice that everything the manager is managing is God's. This becomes important when we realize we are the manager. Everything we have is God's, and we are responsible for using it for the benefit for which God intends. Also in this parable the two things that the manager addresses is olive oil, which is symbolic of the anointing, and wheat, which symbolizes the substance of life. To me this says we are to use our anointing to contribute to life in others.

The second half of the parable gives us probably all the information we need about correctly having and using our Father's riches. **"For the people of this world are more shrewd in dealing with their own kind than are the people of the light. I tell you, use worldly wealth to gain friends for yourselves, so that when it is gone, you will be welcomed into eternal dwellings" (Luke 16:8–9).** First, he tells us the purpose for wealth—taking care of our own kind—and second, he tells us to use worldly wealth for this purpose. It is obvious he intends for us to have worldly wealth; otherwise why would he tell us to use it? But it is in the using that the real secret is found. In the world, the mark of a rich man is the quantity of his possessions. In the kingdom, the mark of a rich man is not what he has, but rather what he gives away.

The secret of kingdom prosperity is in what I referred to as the "sanctity of the relaxed grip." The sanctity of the relaxed grip may be the secret of kingdom prosperity, but knowing and trusting your source is the secret to the sanctity of the relaxed grip. This trusting should be easy when we consider Scriptures such as **2 Corinthians 9:11**, which says, **"You will be made rich in every way so that you can be generous on every occasion."** The sanctity of the relaxed grip simply means we can give whenever the Holy Spirit tells us to, however much he tells us to, and where he tells us to, because we know he will refill our coffers to the top, pressed down and overflowing.

Remember, the counterfeit of heavenly prosperity is worldly commerce, and part of world commerce is to convince us we need everything. No part of the world so fulfills man's lust of the eyes, lust of the flesh, and boastful pride of life as does commercialism. World commerce intended to make us a consumer nation, and it has been very successful. Our worldly "I wanters" are well conditioned to believe that more will make us happier. The commerce of religion has done much to further this false impression. Every day we hear preachers telling us we need more and can get it by buying their books and CDs. Often we ignore important things and deny self-evident truths in our race for riches. *We must never forget that friendship with the world makes us enemies of God.* If we are spending time desiring worldly things and spending our resources to gather them, we are in a dangerous place. If we allow the thought of money to occupy our minds even to a mild obsession, we need to repent and believe God will care for us. We must always remember **"Some people, eager for money, have wandered from the faith and pierced themselves with many griefs" (1 Timothy 6:10).**

We are well advised to listen closely **to Hebrews 13:5–6: "Keep your lives free from the love of money and be content with what you have, because God has said, 'Never will I leave you; never will I forsake you.' So we say with confidence 'The Lord is my helper; I will not be afraid. What can man do to me?'"** Do not lie to yourself about your relationship with worldly things, including money. It will come and it will go, but your security must be in the Lord, not your pocketbook. Your desires to please and to be pleased must be from the Lord, not the world. And who you are must be summed up in Jesus Christ and not your worldly possessions.

I know I have beaten this drum very hard, but I believe that the unrighteous God of Mammon has accounted for more shipwrecked saints than either sex or alcohol. As I have pointed out, God gives us prosperity for a reason. Everything is his and he wants us to enjoy it, but we are to enjoy only part of it; the rest is his witness into the world. If we look at the rest of the parable about the rich man and the dishonest manager, we will see a warning and a promise from God.

> **Whoever can be trusted with very little can also be trusted with much, and whoever is dishonest with very little will also be dishonest with much. So if you have not been trustworthy in handling worldly wealth, who will trust you with true riches? And if you have not been trustworthy with someone else's property, who will give you property of your own? (Luke 16:10–13)**

And **Matthew 6:24** says, **"No servant can serve two masters. Either he will hate the one and love the other, or he will be devoted to the one and despise the other. You cannot serve both God and Money."**

How do we insulate ourselves from becoming overwhelmed by commercialism and at the same time enjoy those things of the world that God wants us to enjoy? First of all, remember we are rich not by what we accumulate but by what we give away. Second of all, listen to the Holy Spirit, and when he says give, give, and when he says enjoy, enjoy. And third, take to heart 1 **Corinthians 7:30–31**, **"… those who buy something, as if it were not theirs to keep; those who use the things of the world, as if not engrossed in them.**

CHAPTER 19

Give and It Shall Be Given

The blessing of the Lord brings wealth, without painful toil for it.

—Proverbs 10:22

One man gives freely, yet gains even more; another withholds unduly, but comes to poverty. *A generous man will prosper; he who refreshes others will himself be refreshed.*

—Proverbs 11:24-25

This historical propensity of God to care for his people plus the Scriptures convinced me of the promise of his prosperity. However, there is no promise of God where individual obedience to the spoken word of the Holy Spirit is more necessary than in this promise of prosperity. Perhaps one could refer to it as faith unto obedience.

Paul argued faith and faith alone. With Peter he won, because Peter's works were of the law and Jewish tradition, but with James it was a different story. James said that without works of the spirit, faith is worthless. James did not talk about blanket obedience to superfluous ordinances. When James said, "You show me your faith and I will show you my works by my faith," he was speaking of the relationship between an individual and the Holy Spirit. Prosperity is ours by faith,

155

but it is only a blessing as we learn to be obedient to the Holy Spirit in the use of our prosperity. You will find no other promise of God that is so conditional as prosperity. In the case of prosperity, that condition is always generosity. For if we are not generous, prosperity becomes a curse—not a curse of God (which does not exist under the New Covenant) but rather a curse of the world system.

We have previously discussed God's propensity to give, and his very nature as a giver. Is it at all surprising, then, that we are called to be givers? **Luke 6:38** says, **"Give, and it will be given to you."** But there is another side of the coin of prosperity. According to 2 Corinthians 8:9, Jesus gave up the riches of heaven and accepted poverty so we could become prosperous. It is this giving up that is also an important part of prosperity. You see, when we give, we are also giving up the resources we could be using for our own flesh. When we are obedient to the Holy Spirit, we are crucifying our flesh and denying our worldly "I wanter." This is what I will refer to as the responsibility of kingdom living—literally death to the old man. I am not going to make a big deal out of this truth, but I believe it is important to see it from God's perspective. Through this giving, he gives us an opportunity to not only exhibit the character of his Son but to seek his will in not befriending the world. Whether we realize it or not, this is also one of the things that leads to prosperity for **"he rewards those who earnestly seek him" (Hebrews 11:6).**

Whenever I am in a conversation about prosperity, not far into the discussion I will be asked, "What about tithing?" My answer is always the same. "I believe tithing is an Old Testament law that brings (like all Old Testament law) condemnation and death. But go ahead and try to keep the law. You never know: you might be the first person ever to be successful." After my sarcasm, we simply change the subject from tithing to the law. Funny thing about this Old Testament law: it is a package deal as it says in **James 2:10–11:**

"For whoever keeps the whole law and yet stumbles at just one point is guilty of breaking all of it. For he who said, 'Do not commit adultery,' also said, 'Do not murder.' If you do not commit adultery but do commit murder, you have become a lawbreaker." Basically, what this is saying is that if you are tithing because God said to tithe, you had better also be setting a kosher table—no more pork—and you better be fulfilling the whole of the Old Testament law, including being circumcised.

Paul spends a certain amount of time speaking about the law in general and circumcision in particular in the fifth chapter of Galatians. **"Again I declare to every man who lets himself be circumcised that he is obligated to obey the whole law" (Galatians 5:3).** Here we see the law as a whole theme again but with a new twist. We are told in Galatians 5:2 that if we are trying to fulfill the law, Christ is of no value to us. **"Mark my words! I, Paul, tell you that if you let yourselves be circumcised, Christ will be of no value to you at all" (Galatians 5:2).** I personally do not believe I am taking too much license if I say that if you are trying to find righteousness in giving by the Old Testament law of tithing, Christ is of no value to you. It's a package deal.

More than forty years ago, I worked for a fund-raising company. I made my living by traveling to congregations throughout the Midwest and putting on a six-week program that aimed to raise the congregation's income by teaching people the value of tithing. I have since repented of my sin, but trust me, I know tithing from both sides and thought I had heard every argument to justify its use. However, I did hear a new one that confused me for a minute. I was told that tithing was not part of the law because it first came through Abraham and not Moses. You will remember that Abraham gave a tenth, which is a tithe, to Melchizedek, which was several hundred years before Moses brought forth the law. Yet as we examine the Scriptures, we find that giving a tenth is declared part of the law in

Hebrews 7:5: "Now the law requires the descendants of Levi who become priests to collect a tenth from the people—that is, their brothers."

Besides being part of the law, there are other things wrong with the concept of tithing. The most quoted Scripture about tithing is **Malachi 3:8–10: "'Will a man rob God? Yet you rob me. But you ask, "How do we rob you?" In tithes and offerings. You are under a curse—the whole nation of you—because you are robbing me. Bring the whole tithe into the storehouse, that there may be food in my house. Test me in this,' says the Lord Almighty, 'and see if I will not throw open the floodgates of heaven and pour out so much blessing that you will not have room enough for it.'"** What people seem to really like about this Scripture is the part about the floodgates of heaven and the pouring out of blessing. A more important part is the part about what happens if you don't bring in the whole tithe and offerings. If you don't fulfill the law completely, you are under a curse. That is clearly stated by the verse above but also by **Galatians 3:10**, which says, **"All who rely on observing the law are under a curse, for it is written: 'Cursed is everyone who does not continue to do everything written in the Book of the Law.'"** But, you proclaim, look at **Galatians 3:13: "Christ redeemed us from the curse of the law by becoming a curse for us, for it is written: 'Cursed is everyone who is hung on a tree.'"** Sorry, you cannot have it both ways. If you want to keep the law of tithing, you are subject to the curse. More important, the tithe is impossible to keep. Let me ask you a question: do you give 10 percent of the gross or of the net? Well, if you do not want to rob God, you should be giving of the gross because you get certain benefits from the money that is taken out of your paycheck. But let's say you are retired. Are you required to pay 10 percent of your Social Security? Well, if you have paid on the gross, you have already paid the tithe on half of your income, but you must pay it on the second half.

Now let's say you go to the grocery store and your bill comes to $50.00 but you have 75 cents' worth of coupons, so your bill is really $49.25. Don't forget to pay your 7.5 cents in tithe. I have been told that is way too picky, that we have a God of grace. I would ask you to look at the words of Jesus as he talks about tithing: **"Woe to you Pharisees, because you give God a tenth of your mint, rue and all other kinds of garden herbs, but you neglect justice and the love of God. You should have practiced the latter without leaving the former undone" (Luke 11:42).** According to Jesus' instruction to those who are under the law, they must give even from what they harvest from their garden down to a precise 10 percent. If we do not keep the law of tithing, we are under the curse, and it is impossible to keep track of everything.

We are New Testament people, and tithing is an Old Testament law. It may surprise you, but there is nowhere in the New Testament that we are asked to tithe. Usually, when I make the above statement, people remind me of the words of Jesus in Luke that I quoted above, where he tells his audience to tithe. Who is his audience? They are Pharisees who live under the law, and according to the law they should be tithing. We, however, are not under the law but are under grace. Another consideration is that the New Testament (New Covenant) had not yet begun when Jesus uttered these words, for his blood, which seals the covenant, had not yet been shed.

The New Testament way is far superior to tithing, for in it there is no judgment and no measure. It is completely about free will and thereby leaves no room for judgment. It is a reward system rather than a condemnation system as in tithing. It is accurately summed up **in Romans 7:6: "But now, by dying to what once bound us, we have been released from the law so that we serve in the new way of the Spirit, and not in the old way of the written code."** The new way of the Spirit is one without condemnation. It is a marvelous concept based not on percentages or numbers or rules

159

but simply on reward. **Luke 6:38 says, "For with the measure you use, it will be measured to you."**

This no-condemnation concept is actually the basis of the whole New Testament, but with our judgmental mind-sets it is hard for us to comprehend. We are told in **Romans 8:1: "Therefore, there is now no condemnation for those who are in Christ Jesus,"** and yet we've failed to completely comprehend it. Nowhere in the New Testament is this no-condemnation/reward system more evident than in the promise of prosperity. As we have pointed out, the Old Testament system of tithing and its demand for exactness was ripe for condemnation and curse. The New Testament system referred to as sowing and reaping is a completely volunteer system where you are rewarded according to your gift and not punished for what you do not give. What a marvelous God we serve, who gives us grace to learn and to grow and to understand. And such a marvelous God is he that if we never learn to serve or grow beyond ourselves or understand the world beyond this world, he still loves and, as we let him, cares for us.

There is a word for this ability of God to give us absolute freedom and to love us no matter how we use it: it is called grace. Grace is another one of those God words that we cannot fully comprehend. It is a purely divine attribute, and in no experience of God is it more evident than in our giving. Grace frees us from the law, from works, and from debt. And then it is so magnificent that it gives us the freedom to go back into the law, to again depend on works and accumulate a debt. Grace is so magnificent that if we ask for it again, it sets us free again. Grace always gives us a choice, and grace rewards us according to our obedience to his Word. But understand: this grace never judges or punishes. Our decision sets in motion cycles of reward or punishment. To the degree that we accept the kingdom's way, we are rewarded, and to the degree that we accept the world's way, we subject ourselves to the world. I guess I would say that the lack of kingdom reward is the world's punishment.

I know that I went down a rabbit trail talking about grace in the middle of a dissertation on prosperity. I also know that nothing has brought grace alive to me more than the difference between Old Testament tithing and New Testament sowing and reaping. I have learned that whenever I feel the urge to give, I immediately try to kick in my grace meter rather than my judgment/condemnation meter. I try to judge not the worthiness of where I believe the Spirit is telling me to give but rather just verify that I've been driven to give by the Spirit and not by emotion or reason. There is no time we are more godlike than when we look at the world through the eyes of grace.

I believe the understanding of tithing as law and the understanding of the law as the enemy of grace-driven Christianity is so important that at the risk of repeating myself, I will sum it up. **"Now the law requires the descendants of Levi who become priests to collect a tenth from the people—that is, their brothers" (Hebrews 7:5).** This Scripture points to the collection of a tenth (the tithe) as part of the law. **"All who rely on observing the law are under a curse" (Galatians 3:10). "You who are trying to be justified by law have been alienated from Christ; you have fallen away from grace" (Galatians 5:4).** There is a better way!

I am a farmer at heart, so sowing and reaping is a pretty easy concept for me to understand, but it actually took me a while to realize why some people did not understand quite as quickly. Another way of expressing it is as seedtime and harvest. As a farmer, one realizes there is a time to plant the seed and then one waits and expects the harvest. Now, quite a bit more goes into raising a crop, such as preparing the field and knowing the right time to plant, but for our purpose, we are going to keep it simple. Besides, God takes care of most of the other stuff.

The seed that you sow is the money that you give. You can call it anything you want, but you do not need nor should you have a calculator to figure it out. You simply need a listening heart. The Holy Spirit will direct you, and later we will talk about some guidelines. The harvest is a little harder to explain. You already have income, so the harvest is that, plus the overflow. Jesus explains this cycle in **Luke 6:38: "Give, and it will be given to you. A good measure, pressed down, shaken together and running over, will be poured into your lap. For with the measure you use, it will be measured to you."** First he gives you the promise "give and it should be given to you." There's simply one condition: you must give. That is the sowing. Then he tells you he will return to you a full bucket, pressed down, shaken together and running over. That is the reaping. Whatever bucket you use after you empty it, he will refill it, then press it in and shake it down, and it will run over. The neat part is that you won't even have to work, because it is going to be poured into your lap, and you don't have a lap unless you are sitting. And it is full of grace, for you get to choose the size of your own bucket and thereby control your own return.

Another way of expressing this is found in **2 Corinthians 9:6**, which says, **"Remember this: Whoever sows sparingly will also reap sparingly, and whoever sows generously will also reap generously."** That is pretty straightforward and self-explanatory. In fact, most of what we need to know about sowing and reaping is found in **2 Corinthians 9**, and as it also contains some unbelievable promises, let us take a look at it.

> **⁶Remember this: Whoever sows sparingly will also reap sparingly, and whoever sows generously will also reap generously. ⁷Each man should give**

what he has decided in his heart to give, not reluctantly or under compulsion, for God loves a cheerful giver. ⁸And God is able to make all grace abound to you, so that in all things at all times, having all that you need, you will abound in every good work. ⁹As it is written:

"He has scattered abroad his gifts to the poor; his righteousness endures forever."

¹⁰Now he who supplies seed to the sower and bread for food will also supply and increase your store of seed and will enlarge the harvest of your righteousness. ¹¹You will be made rich in every way so that you can be generous on every occasion, and through us your generosity will result in thanksgiving to God.

¹²This service that you perform is not only supplying the needs of God's people but is also overflowing in many expressions of thanks to God. ¹³Because of the service by which you have proved yourselves, men will praise God for the obedience that accompanies your confession of the gospel of Christ, and for your generosity in sharing with them and with everyone else.

You will notice I have left the verse numbers in the above Scripture to make it easy to refer to as we look at it line by line. In some instances we may even compare it to verses 8 through 11 of Malachi 3. In verse 6 the Lord exhorts us to remember that our financial future is our choice, whereas in Malachi verse 10, it is a much stronger admonition to bring the whole tithe and to test God. In verse 7 of 2 Corinthians, we are told our giving is a matter of our heart and we are not to be reluctant or to give out of necessity. In Malachi, on the other hand, we are told to bring in the tithe and offerings because it is necessary to please God; if we don't, we are under a curse, and only after we bring in the whole tithe are we subject to any blessing. In Malachi, it is a matter of law, and in 2 Corinthians, it is a matter of free will of the heart. Clearly in this comparison one can see the difference between the Old Testament law and the New Testament grace.

In Malachi, the promises are subject to a very strict and limited ordinance and become operational only when those ordinances are strictly fulfilled. In 2 Corinthians and virtually throughout the New Testament, the requirements are so minimal that in most cases, they require little else than our brief (faith) in them. For instance, take this example of sowing and reaping. Besides our belief, the only requirement is that we give, and it is almost impossible for a Christian to not give somewhere, somehow.

There might be no piece of Scripture that more clearly shows us how overboard God is toward his saints. It is so full of promises that it is hard to find them all and to comprehend them after we find them. But let us take a look, beginning with verse 8. It says God is able to make all grace abound to us. This grace is what motivates us to give in the first place, for it fills us with love, compassion, generosity, and sacrificial willingness. The very nature with which we give comes from God. Then he promises us that we will have all we need to be able to give into every good work. In verse 9 he promises us righteousness. Then we go on to verse 10, where he tells us he furnishes the seed and bread for food. Basically what he's saying is that he supplies our needs and more, so that we have seed to sow. And then he tells us he's going to give us more seed so that we can be more generous. As we are more generous, he promises we will become more righteous. Verse 11 is the granddaddy of all prosperity Scriptures, for it tells us plain up that *we will be made rich in every way.*

Why will we be made rich in every way? Because we have shown that we have the grace to give and that we will be generous on every occasion. Through this generosity, people begin to relate to God, particularly in thanksgiving. Verse 12 tells us our generosity has two results. The first is supplying the needs of God's people, and the second is getting those people to relate to the Father through giving thanks. Verse 13 tells us that we have proved ourselves free from the world of commerce as we profess the good news of Christ's prosperity by our actions. This sowing and reaping thing is unbelievable—and unbelievably simple.

I had a firsthand experience getting people to relate to God through giving. My wife and I often get breakfast at McDonald's, and because we know the employees are often supporting a family and working two jobs, we occasionally, after paying our bill, give the employee a twenty-dollar tip. I did this the other day at each of the windows, and each time the employees said God bless you.

> **With me (wisdom) are riches and honor, enduring wealth and prosperity. My fruit is better than fine gold; what I yield surpasses choice silver. I walk in the way of righteousness, along the paths of justice, bestowing a rich inheritance on those who love me and making their treasuries full. (Proverbs 8:18–21)**

CHAPTER 20

The Ways and Means of Giving

This chapter is going to be kind of a potpourri on giving—not specifically in any one direction, just cleaning up several things I haven't mentioned before.

Whenever I speak on prosperity, someone accuses me of giving to get, also referred to as seeking the blessing. My answer is always the same: it would be a pretty stupid farmer who planted a field and never expected a harvest. For any number of reasons he may never harvest the field, but he would not waste his seed if he did not expect it to germinate and grow. I give as God tells me to, and because I believe God and his Word, I expect to harvest. But let me point out something else that we can learn from the world's commerce: giving is good business. Rich people in the world give. They set up their foundations and reap the world's benefit from it. Know also that the principles of God work whether you are a Christian or not. **Matthew 5:45** says, **"He [your Father] causes his sun to rise on the evil and the good, and sends rain on the righteous and the unrighteous."** I do not understand why, but that's the way it works. I think it's called grace.

If I were to try to describe spiritual giving in secular terms, I would have to say it is not a science; rather it is closer to an emotion. It is not a calculation; rather it is a feeling. Basically, described in spiritual terms, it is listening to and obeying the Holy Spirit. Many of us have a tendency to overlisten to the Holy Spirit, so let me give you some guidelines. You cannot give what you do not have, and you shouldn't give what is not yours to give. As we move from a calculator-driven giving habit to an obedience-driven one, we are prone to making our decisions based on emotion and to actually giving that which is not ours to give. For instance, you pay your electric bill for the electricity you have already used; therefore that money is not yours to give away. Also, you signed an agreement to pay X number of dollars each month for a home mortgage, car loan, or whatever. That money is also not yours to give away. If that money is already accounted for, it is actually not your money; therefore, you should not be giving it away.

To prevent this and also because it's good business, Norma and I live on what we call a zero-balance budget. Basically, that means every cent of income we receive each month is accounted for. We may not spend any particular amount, but it goes into a fund for a particular later purpose. For instance, we do not have a car payment, but we do have a car-replacement account. If I did have a car payment, I would probably have car-payment and car-replacement accounts. That way when I need to replace my car, I will have a significant amount of cash to pay for it. Now of course, the first account I deposit money into is my giving account. This is an amount that the Holy Spirit has placed into my heart and is usually a consistent amount. Next I deposit a certain amount in savings. Then I estimate all of my regular bills and deposit those amounts in the appropriate accounts. After this, I deposit into what I refer to as the contracted accounts—i.e., the house payment, car payment (if I had one), and others such as credit cards. This brings me to what we refer to as living expenses, and from experience we know about how much to deposit into those accounts for things such as groceries, gas, clothing, personal needs, and miscellaneous. Last, we deposit specific amounts into what we call entertainment accounts. These include amounts that are just

Norma's or mine to spend as we please. They also include accounts for dining out, movies, and so on.

Some people keep all these accounts as separate envelopes in their homes, and some actually keep separate bank accounts. Norma and I keep one bank account and maintain where the money is allotted through a spreadsheet. One great advantage of the zero-balance system is that after using it for a while, we generally had an excess at the end of the month. In deciding what to do with this excess, we need to go back and ask the Holy Spirit which of the envelopes to put it in. Usually, we are prompted to just add to the giving account. Sometimes, because he knows the future, God will have us add to another account, and sometimes, just because he is such a generous, wonderful Father, he will tell us to spend it on ourselves. This is an excellent tool for learning to ask, trust, and receive from our Father God.

Norma and I have twenty-two separate accounts. If an account does not have enough money in it to do whatever we want to do, we simply cannot do it. For instance, if we have used up all the money in the dining-out account, we are going to be eating at home. Likewise, if we have given away all the money in the giving account and feel led or compelled to give somewhere, we know it simply will have to wait. We cannot give what we do not have, and we should not give what is not ours to give. **"For if the willingness is there, the gift is acceptable according to what one has, not according to what he does not have. Our desire is not that others might be relieved while you are hard pressed, but that there might be equality" (2 Corinthians 8:12–13).** Always remember, God is not a hard-presser.

I would love to say that this absolutely wonderful financial system was my creation. I cannot say that, however, for it came from a man by the name of Dave Ramsey (www.daveramsey.com). I will add here that I do not agree with all of Mr. Ramsey's views, especially about tithing. But with that said, I will emphasize that I believe the basic principles of Mr. Ramsey's financial program were given to him by God and will assist us in our sojourn through the maze of the world's commerce system.

Most Christians have tremendously generous natures and want to give when they perceive a need. I know for instance that Norma and I have scattered a great deal of seed in the last forty years on the path, on the rocky ground, and among the thorns.

> **A farmer went out to sow his seed. As he was scattering the seed, some fell along the path, and the birds came and ate it up. Some fell on rocky places, where it did not have much soil. It sprang up quickly, because the soil was shallow. But when the sun came up, the plants were scorched, and they withered because they had no root. Other seed fell among thorns, which grew up and choked the plants. (Matthew 13:3–7)**

An examination of the Word will show us that there are specific places where we are asked to give.

High on this list are widows and orphans. **"Religion that God our Father accepts as pure and faultless is this: to look after orphans and widows in their distress and to keep oneself from being polluted by the world" (James 1:27).** This theme is one we see throughout the Old and New Testaments; however, we are also given cautions and instructions in 1 Timothy 5. We are told in **1 Timothy 5:4** to care for our parents: **"But if a widow has children or grandchildren, these should learn first of all to put their religion into practice by caring for their own**

family and so repaying their parents and grandparents, for this is pleasing to God."

Often mentioned in the Word is caring for the poor. The elders in Jerusalem encouraged Paul to remember the poor. **"All they asked was that we should continue to remember the poor, the very thing I was eager to do" (Galatians 2:10)**. I would like to point out, at the risk of offending grace, that if someone is habitually poor, his or her need is not financial but rather is spiritual. Truly, God does not expect us to be poor. I think this may be borne out when we look at **2 Corinthians 8:14–15**, where it says, **"At the present time your plenty will supply what they need, so that in turn their plenty will supply what you need. Then there will be equality, as it is written: 'He who gathered much did not have too much, and he who gathered little did not have too little.'"** Clearly, this Scripture presents a picture of temporary need and calls for equality in the body of Christ. I believe this equality is somewhat geographical. For instance, when I was in Nepal, which is a very poor country, I noticed that the Christians seemed to be living better than those around them. One thing I noticed was that as a whole, the country had little green, but Christians seemed to have more flowers and grass than their non-Christian neighbors. However, when you compared Nepalese Christians' standard of living with North Americans', they would be considered very poor.

Many Christians have a very hard time with the prosperity message. It seems as if they think there is some sanctification in being poor. I do realize there are Scriptures that do not shed good light on rich people. Also, there are Scriptures that talk of the dangers of craving the riches of the world. However, when we examine the Word, we find that God is a rewarding Father who wants his children to be prosperous. When someone is habitually poor in body, soul, or spirit, there is a spiritual problem. It could be as simple as their having a habit of poverty or as complicated as a demon of poverty, but whatever the case, it needs to be dealt with on a spiritual level. To simply keep giving these people a handout is embedding them in their poverty.

We are also encouraged by the Word to support those who bring us the word **(1 Timothy 5:17–18). "The elders who direct the affairs of the church well are worthy of double honor, especially those whose work is preaching and teaching. For the Scripture says, 'Do not muzzle the ox while it is treading out the grain,' and 'The worker deserves his wages'"** This Scripture seems quite clear and plain, but I cannot help but wonder how different the church of today is from the church of the writer of this Scripture. Does the church today resemble more closely the synagogue that the writer was breaking away from than the simple organic fellowship established by the Holy Ghost at Pentecost? The synagogue-type of worship was one of separation. The outer court was open to all who professed certain beliefs, the inner court was limited to only a few, and the Holy of Holies was further limited to a very few elitist professionals. It was a system based upon the belief that there always needed to be a mediator between the common man and God. When Jesus was crucified, the curtain that separated the people from God was torn from top to bottom, and the Holy of Holies that is the place where God resides was opened to all. And in his Son, our Father God declared all believers equal.

It seems evident from the Scriptures that this equality of believers is a very important doctrine of the church, for without it, we will by nature allow the professional churchmen to do the work we are called to do in the body of Christ. There are basically three types of activity that we as members of the body of Christ are to do. They are giftings, services, and workings. The explanation and understanding of how these function in the body is a book in itself, but they find their foundation **in 1 Corinthians 12:4–6: "There are different kinds of gifts, but the same Spirit. There are different kinds**

of service, but the same Lord. There are different kinds of working, but the same God works all of them in all men."

I believe that when we return to a synagogue type, a natural occurrence is for us to no longer be intimately involved in the giftings, services, and workings that are the responsibility of all the people. I also believe that the type that we call church is modeled after the synagogue type. One sign that this is true is the hiring of professional churchmen who oversee our spirituality. When Jesus died, he made us a church of the laity (people) with equality never before experienced in life. Women and slaves were to be considered equal to all, and all were to be considered equal as children of God. A careful examination of the letters to the churches of Ephesus and Laodicea might give us some further insight into what I'm trying to convey. In the letter to the church at Ephesus, the writer commends the church because they hate the practices of the Nicolaitans. The name Nicolaitans is derived from the Greek word *nikolaos,* a compound of the words *nikos* and *laos.* The word *nikos* means "to subdue." The word *laos* is Greek for "the people." It is also where we get the word *laity.* When these two words are compounded into one, they form a word that means "one who subdues the people." Now, this subduing may be intentional or unintentional, but nonetheless, when a person or people in the church are in a position that causes or allows the people—that is, the laity—to no longer feel the need to, or be allowed to, function as equals, you have a church of the Nicolaitans.

Further, let us glance at the letter to the church at Laodicea. Again, we see the word *Laodicea* as made up of two separate words: *laos,* which means "the people," and *dike,* which means "custom" or possibly "the punishment." With this in mind we need to look at **Revelation 3:17–18: "You say, 'I am rich; I have acquired wealth and do not need a thing.' But you do not realize that you are wretched, pitiful, poor, blind and naked. I counsel**

you to buy from me gold refined in the fire, so you can
become rich; and white clothes to wear, so you can cover
your shameful nakedness; and salve to put on your eyes, so
you can see." Maybe we need to ask the Holy Spirit about the
meaning of the gold, the white clothes, and what we are blind to.

Something else very interesting about the letter to the Laodiceans is
found in **verse 20: "Here I am! I stand at the door and knock.
If anyone hears my voice and opens the door, I will come in
and eat with him, and he with me."** Notice that the people are
on the inside of the door but Jesus is on the outside. He is not even
in the church with them. In verse 17 the people declare themselves as
rich and as having acquired wealth and not needing a thing, whereas
Jesus describes them as wretched, pitiful, poor, blind, and naked.
Why does Jesus describe them thusly? It is described plainly in **verse
15 and16: "'I know your deeds, that you are neither cold nor
hot. I wish you were either one or the other! So, because you
are lukewarm—neither hot nor cold—I am about to spit you
out of my mouth.'"** Could this lukewarm state be a result of hiring
someone to be hot in place of us?

I know that I have gone far afield to simply say that I am not sure
the writer of the Scripture that exhorts us to support "the elders
who direct the affairs of the church well" had in mind or was even
able to imagine the type that we call church today. I do not believe
the writer could have imagined a building on every corner with
professional staff to direct our every spiritual thought when writing
this Scripture. However, that is for you and the Holy Spirit to decide.

As for me, I have been involved for more than ten years in what I
consider a better way. I have been involved with basically the same
small group of people for more than ten years, meeting and breaking
bread on a regular basis and involving ourselves in each other's lives as
equals. We have no building, no pastor (although we do have people

who are pastoral), and no collection. We have no sermon; rather we have a dialogue in which all participate. No one is predominant, and everyone answers to all.

I certainly do not believe that I have mentioned every place where the Holy Spirit will direct us to give, but I can find no place in the New Covenant where we are to be giving to the maintenance of a building. Enough said!

Do you know Christians who have what we refer to as the Midas touch? Everything they put their hand to makes money. They have extraordinary abundance and they live an extraordinary life, but they have also an extraordinary responsibility. They are God's channel through which he provides funding for specific needs. **"If a man's gift is ... contributing to the needs of others, let him give generously" (Romans 12:6–8).**

I have known several of these people in my walk, and I have watched them live extraordinary lives and have watched them become ordinary. What I'm about to say is just my opinion: when these people are listening to the Word of God, be it directly from the Holy Spirit or the prophetic word to someone else, they are blessed with extraordinary blessing. But when these same people make rules by which to give, the extraordinary blessings seem to disappear.

I will give you an example. Many years ago, I was slightly involved with a situation in which a young woman came to a husband and wife who had this service of money and asked for help. The story is a little more complicated than this, but the simplicity of it is that another man came to the husband and told him that the young woman really had no needs and was being taken care by God. This was a prophecy from the Holy Spirit. The husband looked squarely at the man and said, "We have been blessed and have told God that whenever somebody has a need, we will give." This man's rules overruled God's word that the young woman really did not have a need. By contributing to the young woman, they actually allowed her to continue in dangerous sin.

The epilogue of the story is that the husband, who had a very well-paying position in the community, was demoted, soon left his job altogether, and had to move to another state to find employment. As far as I know, after a brief bump in the road these people are maybe in a better place than before. (Isn't God's grace wonderful?) My contact with this couple has been minimal in the last few years, so I do not know whether or not they connected the dots and learned from the above situation. I do know they remain incredibly generous people. I know the above situation and several others have showed me a lot about the responsibility of the gift of generosity.

The people with this servicing it seems to me are called to a high level of listening to the Holy Spirit, for if they give correctly, they are the hand of God, but if they give incorrectly, much damage can be done. I once had a gentleman with this servicing tell me, "When I give to such-and-such, my stocks do well, but when I give to that place, my stocks go down." My answer to him was quite simply that I would give to the former and stop giving to the latter. Because this ministry is so important, it seems to me that it requires an extraordinary measure of humility, patience, and wisdom. I do not believe we can ever properly function in this ministry by following a set of rules.

True godly prosperity is far more than money. Simply, by showing up as a baby, Jesus Christ guaranteed us a prosperous soul and a rich relationship with our heavenly Father. Many Christians struggle very hard with this message of prosperity. Somehow, it seems ingrained deep within us that we should be poor. It is hard for me to reconcile this mind-set with the entire Word of God. For instance, **Matthew 20:15** says, **"Don't I have the right to do what I want with**

my own money? *Or are you envious because I am generous?"* **(Emphasis mine.)** Jesus is telling the parable, and in the parable the landowner is his Father God, whom he clearly refers to as generous. Maybe I would be forced to ask those who resist the prosperity message the same question Jesus asked in the parable: are you envious because my Father God is generous?

I carry this prosperity theme so far that I believe, as was the experience of the Israelites in the desert, that our things should not wear out or break or cause us problems. That does not mean that we should not have new things, but we should get them because we want new things and not because the old things wore out. Think how fantastic it is to sell or give something to someone that is as blessed as our possessions should be blessed. I must comment, though, that since I have been writing this chapter on prosperity, nearly everything we own has broken or needed repair of some kind. My wife said, "Enough: finish the chapter."

I like prosperity; it is one of my favorite promises. I have absolutely no problem believing God wants me to be prosperous when I read Scriptures such as **Romans 8:32: "He who did not spare his own Son, but gave him up for us all—how will he not also, along with him, graciously give us all things?"** I also wholly believe that he wants you prosperous if you believe.

Psalm 112:1-10

> **Praise the Lord.**
> **Blessed is the man who fears the Lord,**
> **who finds great delight in his commands.**
> **His children will be mighty in the land;**
> **the generation of the upright will be blessed.**
> **Wealth and riches are in his house,**
> **and his righteousness endures forever.**

Even in darkness light dawns for the upright,
for the gracious and compassionate and righteous
man.
Good will come to him who is generous and lends
freely,
who conducts his affairs with justice.
Surely he will never be shaken;
a righteous man will be remembered forever.
He will have no fear of bad news;
his heart is steadfast, trusting in the LORD.
His heart is secure, he will have no fear;
in the end he will look in triumph on his foes.
He has scattered abroad his gifts to the poor,
his righteousness endures forever;
his horn will be lifted high in honor.

CHAPTER 21

My Ordeal

In August 2013, commencing coincidentally with my starting the chapters on science and health, after what we think was about fifteen years of having no need to see a doctor, I began to feel bad. In a month's time, I was getting progressively worse. I asked for prayer and anointing by the elders of my fellowship. Nothing seemed to help, and the symptoms were evasive and progressive. By asking for prayer, I drew attention to myself, and my family began to watch me like a hawk. My son-in-law and I meet every Thursday morning for breakfast. During one of these breakfasts my son-in-law said, "You need to go home and do nothing all day but rest." That evening my son noticed my speech was slightly slurred and was greatly concerned. In our discussions my wife and I came to three considerations. (1) It was probably pride and fear that kept me from the doctor, neither of which are godly emotions; (2) with the level of anxiety my children and grandchildren were experiencing, maybe love dictated that I should put my pride and fear aside; (3) I needed to decide, if I went to a doctor, who it should be. My wife's doctor, Gretchen, who is actually a physician's assistant, was a family friend of more than thirty years—someone who I knew understood my faith and loved me.

At this point, I knew I had to do something, so I said I would go see Gretchen. My wife called the clinic where she works and they said her schedule was filled that day. My wife said, "Tell Gretchen it's

178

Chuck, and somewhat of an emergency" and Gretchen said I should come right down.

I was in her office perhaps ten minutes when she looked at me and said, "Chuck I want to admit you to the emergency room. Will you go?" I said yes. They admitted me to the hospital with blood pressure of 240 on the high side and 145 on the low side. Their protocol of course was to immediately lower my blood pressure and stabilize it. They were very successful in lowering it; however, they could not keep it down, which in retrospect may have saved my life. To the surprise of pretty much everyone, they discharged me from the hospital that evening. I was very glad to be discharged, but after I got home and began to feel weird, I told my wife I did not feel safe and needed to return to the hospital, which we did.

I need to inject something else into this story. About two weeks earlier I had told my wife one night that I was feeling and seeing demons in the house. We of course rebuked them and covered the house with the blood of Christ. It was this same attacking, weird presence I felt when I came home from the hospital. When I returned to the hospital, I felt safe and the staff was absolutely great. I felt cared for. The downside was that they were monitoring my blood pressure closely and woke me every few minutes all night to check it, so I got very little sleep. We all stayed at the hospital that night. My son slept in a chair in my room, and my daughter and wife slept on cots in a lounge. Wednesday night was a repeat of Tuesday night, and I received very little sleep. Wednesday morning I was exhausted and discouraged. I had just drifted off to sleep when a technician came into the room for yet another test. My son tried in vain to persuade the technician to allow me to sleep, but she had her schedule to keep. As it turned out, this should have been a very easy test, a simple EKG. However, because of my exhausted state and because of the peculiar way she contorted me in the bed, it was a very long forty-five minutes.

The day was filled with tests, so again I got no rest. As night approached, I was exhausted, and my children had gone home. My wife and I had just settled in for a good night's sleep, when four nurses rushed into the room, startling us both awake. Apparently, my heart monitor had briefly flatlined and would not return to a steady rhythm. As this regional hospital had no cardiac care unit, they were going to transfer me to a cardiac unit about forty miles away. I had a very nice ambulance ride, and immediately upon my arrival at that hospital, they determined by some simple physical tests that I had actually had a stroke. They were going to leave my blood pressure alone, completely reversing the protocol from the previous hospital. The bright spot was that they were no longer taking my blood pressure every few minutes, so I did get a great night's sleep and felt quite good. Thursday was definitely a turning point, as the results of the numerous tests begin to come back. We began to catch snatches of conversation here and there that let us know more precisely where we were at and where we were going from there. For instance, it was confirmed I had had some strokes at some point and that there was some damage, although we did not know how much. Also we learned that there was some blockage of the left internal carotid artery.

I realize this does not sound all that positive, but when you know nothing, any news helps. The staff at this hospital was as wonderful and charming as they were at the previous one, and I was very comfortable, especially because I had had some rest. Thursday, believe it or not, consisted of even more tests. I had already had an MRI, and now they were giving me an MRA. We were straightforward and honest with the staff of both hospitals: we told them we were Christians and that our decisions would be based upon that, and that we felt that somewhere, there would be a line in the sand when we would say, "Enough; no more." We were pleasantly surprised at how well that stand was understood and respected. The other thing I had said from the beginning was that I needed to be out of the hospital by Friday night. My three oldest grandchildren were performing together in a benefit concert, and I was not going to miss it. Also, I had a date with my youngest granddaughter on Saturday. Her older sister, mother, aunt, and cousin were leaving her behind, as they were going to a concert in Minneapolis with backstage tickets to meet the boys of Big Time Rush. I did not want Lily to feel left out, so her grandma and I were going to meet some dogs of the breed that I was interested in purchasing. A wonderful, gracious lady had agreed to share her three Bouviers with us, and then we were going to an amusement park for the rest of the day.

Well, late on Thursday, we finally met my doctor. Dr. Snyder is a neurologist. We immediately liked him and trusted him. Dr. Snyder said with a certain amount of credulousness in his voice that what he was seeing in me was not what he expected. In other words, I was not supposed to be in near as good a shape as I was according to the results of the MRI. Eventually he said it was a miracle. The doctor said they knew my left interior carotid artery was at least partially blocked and my right interior carotid artery was good. What he assumed was happening and the reason there was not more brain damage, other than a miracle, was that my high blood pressure actually pushed the blood from the right to the left. He further told us that there was nothing they could do to alleviate the blockage. But he also said he wanted to do one more MRI to see how extensive the blockage was. Present for this conference was my son, daughter, and son-in-law. It was like the Holy Spirit spoke to all of our hearts at the same time and said no more tests. My son expressed this to the doctor and said, "Why would we have that test? You already said nothing could be done." He asked, "What if you find out it's 100 percent blocked? Will you do anything different?" The doctor answered no. "What if you find out it is only 40 percent blocked?" The doctor said no. Finally, when pressed, the doctor said the test would only be for his information and might assist in the future for someone else's treatment. I suggested that I am not a very good guinea pig, but if the doctor wanted to do the test, it was okay with me. But my children were universally against the test, and the doctor agreed not to do it.

Having woken up from another decent night's sleep, I was in a good mood, especially considering the consensus from the night before that we were finished with tests. I was greeted that morning by news from the nurse that the doctor had ordered another test. I informed her that the patient was not having another test until the doctor justified it to me. She assured me I needed this test. I assured her it was not going to happen until I saw the doctor. The physician's assistant, whom we liked a lot, came in and tried to convince me but to no avail. Eventually, the neurologist came by, and it took him about thirty seconds to convince me I would take the test. The doctor explained that it was what's called a chemical stress test.

They put me through a machine that took pictures of my heart at rest. Then they gave me a radioactive chemical that would give them good pictures of my heart, and another chemical that made my heart work very hard. Again they put me through the machine and took pictures of my heart at work. Comparing the pictures told them what shape my heart was in. The doctor wanted to leave the blood pressure high, but to do that, he needed to know that the heart was in good shape. Otherwise, he said, I could die from a heart attack at any time. He said, "We can't do anything about the blockage in the brain; however, we can do a lot of things to fix the heart if it needs it." I immediately sent a text to all the people in my group to pray very hard for the next four hours. Apparently when all was said and done, this was really the only test that counted.

The next several hours were very stressful, but I did feel a heavenly presence through it all. The technician who gave me the test twice was great. I believe his name was Steve. It seemed like a very long time before we knew the results of the stress test. When it seemed we could wait no longer, one of my children saw Renee, our beloved physician's assistant, in the hall, and she said everything looked great. A little later, she practically danced into the room and gave us the news that my heart was in good shape and didn't require stents or anything. She then said she was going to put in the order for my discharge so I could make it home in time to shower and get to the concert. Shortly after that, my neurologist came to the room and with his outstanding, positive bedside manner assured me everything was going to be okay.

It appears that one of the side effects of a stroke is that you become quite emotional. I have been a tough old cowboy, carefully hiding my emotions most of my life. Now, if someone happened to mention someone's kitty had died three states away, I would burst out crying and struggle to control myself. We live in a pretty small community, and my wife in her infinite wisdom realized there would be a lot of people at this concert who had no idea what had happened to me and that just saying, "Hi, Chuck" could set me off on a cry. Because we had balcony seats, we decided we would wait till the last minute and a friend would go with me through the lobby and up the stairs; then I would be safe. I made it fine, and the kids performed wonderfully. My ten-year-old grandson Charlie is not just a ham; he is a whole ham sandwich complete with mayo and lettuce. Shortly before intermission, I left to avoid the crowds.

Saturday also went well, but Lily was a little intimidated by the size of the dogs, although they were very gentle with her and Grandpa was not a lot of fun at the amusement park. Fortunately, Lily's older cousin Charlie, whom she idolizes, went with us, and that helped a lot. As we were getting ready to leave, Lily said she wanted to do one more ride. I said, "Go ahead. Grandma will take you, and I'll go sit in the car." When they got to the amusement, the line was quite long and only two were allowed in at a time. Lily looked at the ride, looked at the line, and said, "I can do this some other time, Grandma. Grandpa is tired, and we need to go."

I have been out of the hospital for a month and am still figuring out what my body needs to heal and how much healing it actually needs. But a far tougher fight has been the healing of my soul. I tend to be a very black-and-white individual who does not thrive spiritually in a gray garden. My supposition in this book is quite simply that we must believe God and he promises us five things: eternal salvation; that we will be filled with his spirit; holiness; health; and prosperity. I think I have provided Scriptures to support each thing I contended, and I believe I did it with full conviction, perhaps even degrading those who don't believe as I do and failing to understand how people cannot understand. However, after my ordeal, regardless of the reason for it, I was having trouble justifying my beliefs. Where before everything was black and white and I was sure of what I believed, now I still believed, but it was fuzzy with doubt.

I found myself doing something I had never before considered. I found myself hoping that the entire Bible is true. Otherwise, what would make us think any of it is true? Take for instance **Psalm 103:2–5:**

> **Praise the Lord O my soul,**
> **and forget not all his benefits—**
> **who forgives all your sins**
> **and heals all your diseases,**
> **who redeems your life from the pit**
> **and crowns you with love and compassion,**
> **who satisfies your desires with good things**
> **so that your youth is renewed like the eagle's.**

The Word says forget not all his benefits, and it lists first, as it should, that he forgives all our sins. I must believe that; otherwise our whole existence is one of foolishness. The next benefit listed is that he heals all our diseases. If the first is true, the second must be also.

Armed with this logic, I considered my choices. One was to give up the project, but as I believe the Holy Spirit directed me to begin the project, it is not in me to give it up. Second, I could rewrite it, but as I reread some of the material, I still agreed with it, and a rewrite would simply be saying the same thing in a different way. As I reread some of what I wrote, I had to admit I still believed, although my experience didn't agree at all with it. It was the believing that counted, not the experience. I would say that if the Scriptures are true, then my experience must be a lie.

Suddenly, I found myself agreeing with Emily Dickinson and understanding what she meant in the poem "Hope Is the Thing with Feathers."

"Hope" is the thing with feathers—
That perches in the soul—
And sings the tune without the words—
And never stops—at all—

I am well aware that my narrow interpretation of Scripture is simply one view, albeit the correct one. Nowhere is this more evident than in my own family. My son-in-law views medicine simply as a tool. My answer to that is that a gun is a tool, too, but you need to know when and how to use it or it is very dangerous. My son's view of the world and what is and what is not evil, on the other hand, is very different from mine. And he is as sure that he is right as I am, so we just agree to disagree. My daughter agrees more with my parochial, narrow view in interpreting Scripture, particularly in relation to medicine. And her views went a long way toward healing my soul. She simply did not understand why my faith was injured because I submitted to science. I paraphrase her expression of how she viewed my ordeal: "You are not alive today because medicine saved you; you are alive today because faith protected you" and "We have talked about the battles between good and evil; you just went through a battle between faith and science, and the scientist [doctor] declared faith the winner when he declared you a miracle."

Actually I felt good about what I had written up to this point, except the next chapter was a less-than-flattering exposé of the medical community, and I thought I would have to at least rewrite that. But as I reread it and think of my own experience, I believe my experience validates what I wrote. When I was admitted to the first hospital, they assumed my problem was high blood pressure and treated that. The doctors at the next hospital diagnosed my problem as stroke and said my high blood pressure was probably what stopped the deterioration of my brain, and they reversed the treatment of high blood pressure. Actually, the first hospital by drastically lowering my blood pressure could have killed me, and my cause of death would have been listed as heart attack caused by high blood pressure, or stroke caused by high blood pressure.

There is something I need to clarify about the next chapter. The people in medicine have the same motivation as the people in faith healing: to alleviate pain and suffering. I say this to celebrate the excellent care I received during my stay in both hospitals. It was quickly evident that my caregivers both cared and gave. I always felt loved and cared for. I encountered very little of the arrogance that I have in the past associated with the medical profession. I always felt that as our family made our beliefs evident, they were respected and appreciated.

CHAPTER 22

Health

Praise the Lord, O my soul; all my inmost being, praise his holy name. Praise the Lord, O my soul, and forget not all his benefits—who forgives all your sins and heals all your diseases.

—Psalm 103:1–3

Recently, I overheard a conversation between two men. The first asked the second if he was healthy, wealthy, and wise. The second man replied that he guessed he was wealthy enough and maybe sometimes wise, but if he could choose only one, he would take healthy, because without his health, the other two wouldn't matter. Although I agree with the sentiment, I take exception to our methods of achieving this sought-after health. We are a nation obsessed with health and are attempting to bankrupt ourselves and our nation to achieve it. And all the time it is simply a promise of God, free for the asking and believing.

I may tend to rant and rave a little in this chapter, for I believe as ministers of this gospel of healing that we tend to be faithless cowards. We tend to be as addicted to the medical community as the unbelieving world around us. It seems to me we should be humiliated enough, considering our rate of infidelity in marriage is about the same as the world's, our divorce rate is the same, our addictions are the same, and we suffer from the same demons. But add to this the fact that we are seeking the same medical cures as the world, dying of the same diseases, and being murdered by medical malpractice at the same rate as the world, and it makes me wonder if we should not rethink our Christianity.

In this passage, Jesus is confronted with a similar situation: **"'O unbelieving and perverse generation,' Jesus replied, 'how long shall I stay with you? How long shall I put up with you? Bring the boy here to me.' Jesus rebuked the demon, and it came out of the boy, and he was healed from that moment"** (Matthew 17:17–18).** The disciples were brave enough to ask Jesus why they could not heal the boy, and **"He replied, 'Because you have so little faith'" (Matthew 17:20).** I can almost hear the chorus of protests rising out there in the hinterlands. Trust me, I've heard all the excuses and used some of them myself. Is it not about time we woke up?

We have support groups and twelve-step programs for just about every weakness known to man. What all of these groups have in common is that first you must admit you have a problem. Why can we not admit we have an impotent Christianity and find a support group? "Hello, my name is Chuck and I'm an impotent Christian, and I shall remain an impotent Christian until I see the failure of the world to meet my needs and begin to trust God and only God."

A support group is first of all for daily accountability, second for celebration of victory, and last of all for encouragement in failure. To be effective, a support group must have a defined purpose. It is a rifle approach to a problem rather than a shotgun approach. The importance to one's life of the purpose and approach must be acknowledged by all. Above all, honesty must prevail.

You might be wondering why I'm talking about support groups in the middle of a dissertation on health. Well, you remember me discussing our need for eight to twelve other people. I believe if we really want to grow spiritually, this is certainly a way to get it done. If we allow God to bring these people into our lives, we will find accountability, celebration, and encouragement, and a safe haven for our faith to grow. There are a couple of prerequisites. We must let the group grow organically. By that I mean we must not set a predetermined agenda, such as a Bible study group, or a church doctrine discussion group, or a group to discuss last Sunday's sermon. Do not allow anyone to be a dominant leader and you will find that the Holy Spirit will lead you in adventures of faith. Also, we must have patience—with ourselves, each other, and the Holy Ghost. Remember, above all this group is about discovering who we are, and not what we have done or what we can do. If we find out who we are, the "doing" of Christianity will come naturally and not be the result of a religious compulsion.

As I mentioned before, America is obsessed with its health. According to the National Public Radio report called "Health Care in America: Follow the Money" by Natalie Jones of March 19, 2012, the average amount spent on health care per individual per year in 1970 was $356. In 2010, the average amount spent on health care per individual per year was $8,402. What we would naturally say is that a dollar in 2010 is worth more than a dollar in 1970. However, according to the website www.measuringworth.com/ppowerus/, the $356 in 1970 would be worth $2,000–$4,970 in 2010. If we ventured to use a number near the top of the range, what this tells us is that we are spending nearly twice as much per individual per year on health care. Much of this cost is subsidized by our employers or the government, but the bottom line is, it is cost.

According to the same article, there are other indicators of how obsessed we have become with our health. Almost one-third of all professional degrees are in health care, and the health-care-related workforce is the third highest after only retail and wholesale. These numbers do not include people who work for pharmaceutical or health insurance companies.

But the most alarming statistic of all is that in 1970, 7.2 percent of our gross national product was spent on health care, we are presently at nearly 18 percent, and this is expected to nearly double in the next ten years, especially with the government now involved. To put this into perspective, it is about 40 percent higher than other industrialized nations. This trend is not sustainable, and no matter how we confront it from a worldly perspective, it's a highway to financial disaster.

It seems to me there's no doubt we are a nation obsessed and that our attitudes toward health care have changed drastically since 1970. I believe two human emotions have propelled this drive: fear and hope. Since 1970, the amount of advertising dollars spent on health care products has risen exponentially. These advertisements have instilled in us a fear of disease and given us at the same time false hope that the products advertised will keep us safe, make us beautiful, and keep us potent. I find it absolutely amazing that in a thirty-second spot, more than half of it is spent telling us about the side effects and dangers involved in taking the cure, yet we ignore them in the hopes that whatever medicine is advertised will be our savior. We are, through Internet and TV advertising, a very educated nation. Give me a pain or symptom, and I can figure out at least two or three horrible diseases that I am probably dying from. And I know that if I hurry to the doctor and catch it early, my chances of survival are greater—all the time ignoring the fact that Jesus said he will protect us from the diseases that come upon the world.

I have been told I have a great faith and that that is why I can survive without the medical community. My reply to this statement is simply that I believe my faith is no more than normal. If you depend upon the medical community, I believe your faith is abnormal. The reason I do not go to doctors has less to do with faith and more to do with fear. When the statistics are looked at from a reasonable perspective, I don't know how one can go to science for medical answers.

In this age of information neither the Centers for Disease Control, The American Medical Association, nor The National Medical Association report medical error as a cause of death. However, if you want to do the research, you can extrapolate the information.

For instance, I quickly came across an article about this, which was as interesting for the information it contained as it was for who had authored it. This article was published in the *Philadelphia Inquirer* on April 25, 2011, and was written by David Cole and Kathleen Sibelius, former secretary of Health and Human Services. After briefly discussing the great medical care in America, the article goes on to point out that the Institute of Medicine estimates that as many as 100,000 Americans die each year from preventable medical errors in hospitals, which is about the number of annual deaths caused by auto accidents, AIDS, and breast cancer combined.

This 100,000 deaths by medical error is a number put forth in 1984 from a study done by the Institute of Medicine. First decried by the medical community it is now ubiquitously used. However it is not really substantiated by the evidence. Investigation leads most to believe the number is actually significantly higher. For instance in a piece titled "More Treatment, More Mistakes" published in the opinion pages of the *New York Times,* July 31, 2012, Sanjay Gupta, the associate chief of neurosurgery at Grady Memorial Hospital and the chief medical correspondent for CNN makes several very interesting assertions and presents many theories pertinent to our thoughts.

He asserts that a reasonable estimate of the number of patients killed by medical mistakes is 200,000 Americans per year, making medical error the third leading cause of death after cancer and heart attack. He further asserts that this staggering number is caused at least in part by doctors overprescribing medicines and procedures and that this overprescribing is done to protect doctors from lawsuits.

Basically, Dr. Gupta is saying that the reason doctors are ordering so many unnecessary tests that could possibly harm patients is to prevent themselves from being sued. So it's the lawyers' fault. Oh yes, the reason we cannot know for sure how many medical mistakes there are is that not all states record them in the same way. Where is the professional accountability when all we do is hide our mistakes, or in some cases bury them, and blame others?

What if Dr. Gupta's theory is wrong? What if the motivation for so many tests and prescriptions that could possibly harm patients is profit? How we could ever believe that the marriage of insurance and medical practice is a good idea is beyond me. But know something, because your life could depend on it: the medical industry is driven by profit. In the medical community, science and commerce have become one. This board of directors answering to stockholders is determining your medical care.

Medicine is big business. I live in a city of 12,000 surrounded by smaller cities half that size all within fifteen minutes, and all have large hospitals full of very expensive equipment. That means there are four hospitals within fifteen minutes of my home plus several well-equipped clinics. Within fifty minutes of my home is a large metropolitan area with at least three huge hospitals, one a university teaching hospital. At some level in every one of these institutions, profit becomes the driving force.

I can already feel the criticism beginning, but please do not misunderstand: I appreciate the medical community for the unsaved, for they have nothing else. But if we are Christians, we do! The promises are clear, the examples are prevalent, and the choice is ours. Let's take a look at those promises.

CHAPTER 23

Healed

Is any one of you sick? He should call the elders of the church to pray over him and anoint him with oil in the name of the Lord. And the prayer offered in faith will make the sick person well; the Lord will raise him up. If he has sinned, he will be forgiven. Therefore confess your sins to each other and pray for each other so that you may be healed. The prayer of a righteous man is powerful and effective.

—James 5:14–16

Okay, that last chapter was boring, although maybe necessary. Let's move on to something more exciting. The above Scripture gives us very specific instructions for what to do when we are not well. It would seem to me to take any other course of action would be being disobedient, yet rarely do we ever follow its instructions. Does God punish us for this disobedience? I do not believe so, for the disobedience becomes its own punishment. Let me explain. Anytime we go to the world instead of believing the Word of God, it is going to cost us financially, emotionally, and painfully. The world delivers its own punishment like its ruler: its only objective is to rob, to steal, and to kill.

Before proceeding, I must insert a disclaimer: I am not a Greek scholar; in fact, I have struggled in the past to spell the words *Greek* and *scholar*. I'm a very simple man with a very limited education. My expertise in Greek is limited to basically two books, Zondervan's *Interlinear Greek-English New Testament* and *Expository Dictionary of New Testament Words* by W. E. Vine, published by Revell. With that said, let us proceed.

I believe this Scripture from James presents us with a conundrum. First of all, if it means what we traditionally believed it to mean, we condemn ourselves by not following its instructions. However, I do not think it means what we traditionally have believed it to mean. I think this is a perfect example of a donkey load of sticks (see earlier chapter). The Greek words used in James for *sick* are not the common word for *illness* in the Greek. The first word is *astheneo* and is translated "sick," but the actual meaning is much closer to "weak" or "feeble." The second word used is *kamno,* which is the effect of too much work on the body. A much closer translation of James 5:14–15 might be that when one becomes exhausted, be it from physical labor, spiritual labors, spiritual discouragement, or sin, we are to call the elders, not run to the doctors, psychologists, or chiropractors. We may gain more insight by looking at **Hebrews 12:3: "Consider him who endured such opposition from sinful men, so that you will not grow weary and lose heart."** The word translated *weary* in Hebrews 12 is the same word translated as *sick* in James.

Sometimes I confuse myself. A couple of chapters ago, I was saying maybe we condemn ourselves by not obeying James 5:14–15. Now I'm saying maybe that same Scripture does not mean what we think it means. Am I letting us off the hook? Not in the least! In fact, I think I'm about to muddy the waters even more.

The normal Greek word for *sick* is *nosos*. Except for an out-of-context use in 1 Timothy 6:4, this word does not appear anywhere in the epistles. This leads me to believe that sickness was so foreign to the early church, they did not even talk of it. Right away someone is going to bring up the case of Epaphroditus, whom Paul describes in Philippians 2:26–27 as having almost died in the work of Christ. It is said in the Scripture that he was ill, but the word used for *ill* is the same word used in James for *weak, feeble,* or *exhausted.* Actually, I think when we read Philippians 2:26–27 in that context, it makes more sense.

Next, we would point to Galatians 4:13, where Paul talks of his own infirmity. The word translated is *illness,* but it is the same word used above for *weary.* I believe it is also safe to assume that he is speaking of the same incident in 2 Corinthians 12:7 when he speaks of a thorn in his flesh to keep him from being puffed up. There is no real indication that these situations involved physical illness, and certainly *nosos* does not appear in either text. As an aside, maybe if Paul had called the elders, asked them to pray over him, and confessed his propensity toward pride as sin, he would have been healed. Of course, maybe he was too proud to do that—*just saying.*

Why is it so hard to believe that the early church did not consider sickness? You had men such as Peter, whose very shadow healed people (Acts 5:15). Yes, you say, but he was an apostle, so of course he could heal. But then we have men such as Philip, who performed great signs and miracles (Acts 8:13), and Stephen, a man full of God's grace and power, who did great wonders and miraculous signs among the people (Acts 6:8). The traditions of the early church are full of stories of such men. Then we must consider the ministry of Jesus, who spent much time and effort relieving men, women, and children of sickness. Why would it be any different today? If he was so interested in conquering evil and relieving the pain and suffering of people 2,000 years ago, would he not be equally interested today? He said that whatever things he did, we would do even greater things (John 14:12), people; I'm just not seeing it.

So here is my supposition: because 2,000 years ago Jesus Christ took a beating, we do not have to be sick. **First Peter 2:24 says, "By his wounds you have been healed."** Now people will probably act in one of three ways, considering this theory. There are those who will simply dismiss it because it does not agree with their theology. A second group will receive it completely because it does agree with their theology. But a third will think it's interesting, although they don't know one way or the other. For them, I will try to produce more evidence for my outrageous claim.

I have spoken earlier of what I call the "segmentation of the visitation." First Peter 2:24 is a example of that. It clearly says that because he was wounded, we are healed. Here is a quote from **Isaiah 53:4–5: Surely he took up our infirmities ... and ... by his wounds we are healed.** Typically, if I believe the Holy Spirit is telling me some principle of God, I will look to the Old Testament for confirmation. I will look to see if there are examples of God dealing with his people in a similar way in the past. I truly believe the Old Testament is given to us as a type and an example of how God deals with his people, albeit not always exactly in a parallel way.

When considering the principle of healing, one Scripture definitely comes to mind:

> **Then Moses cried out to the Lord, and the Lord showed him a piece of wood. He threw it into the water, and the water became sweet. There the Lord issued a ruling and instruction for them and put them to the test. He said, "If you listen carefully to the Lord your God and do what is right in his eyes, if you pay attention to his commands and keep all his decrees, I will not bring on you any of the diseases I brought**

> ## on the Egyptians, for I am the Lord, who heals you." (Exodus 15:25–26)

There is probably no scriptural segment that more closely parallels our exodus from the world system into the kingdom system than the story of the Israelites' exodus from Egypt into the Promised Land after 400 years of slavery. The above Scripture is part of that story. The Israelites had been in the desert for three days without water. When they found water, it was bitter and undrinkable. So understandably, they did what most of us do when we find ourselves in a bitter, dry place. They forgot what God had just done in the past and complained about the present, unable to see any future. Because he was the leader and also maybe because he feared for his own well-being, Moses cried out to the Lord. God then showed him a piece of wood. For some reason Moses deemed it wise to throw it into the water, and lo and behold, the water became sweet. There is a great lesson right here for us: whenever we have a bitter situation, the only remedy is the wood. Of course, that is a reference to the cross of Christ, but it also refers to our cross.

Please allow me to digress for a moment. Much ado is made about what our cross is. I personally believe that it is giving up our humanity and picking up our spirituality, something that is very hard to do in the world. This moving from carnality to spirituality is a moment-to-moment experience. I would use four Scriptures to press my point. **Philippians 3:18–20: "For, as I have often told you before and now say again even with tears, many live as enemies of the cross of Christ. Their destiny is destruction, their god is their stomach, and their glory is in their shame. Their mind is on earthly things. But our citizenship is in heaven."** This Scripture tells us clearly where our mind should not be and where our citizenship is. It also tells us that if we are carnal— that is, worldly—and consider doing things only as the world does, we may be an enemy of the cross of Christ.

The next Scripture we should consider for a moment is **Galatians 6:14: "May I never boast except in the cross of our Lord Jesus Christ, through which the world has been crucified to me, and I to the world."** Generally speaking we think of the cross as the instrument that has forgiven us of our sins and saved us eternally. Rarely do we consider it the instrument of victory over the world in our lives. No wonder, considering what the cross cost our heavenly Father and our Lord Jesus Christ, they consider us enemies of that cross when we live carnally in the world. Remember **James 4:4: "You adulterous people, don't you know that friendship with the world means enmity against God? Therefore, anyone who chooses to be a friend of the world becomes an enemy of God."**

With the above scriptures in mind, let's take a new look at an old Scripture:

> **Then he said to them all: "Whoever wants to be my disciple must deny themselves and take up their cross daily and follow me. For whoever wants to save their life will lose it, but whoever loses their life for me will save it. What good is it for someone to gain the whole world, and yet lose or forfeit their very self?" (Luke 9:23–25)**

It seems to me that the connection between these Scriptures and the message they convey is self-evident—namely, that we are to deny ourselves the world's way and begin to think of ourselves not as carnal or human but as spiritual beings who are citizens not of this earth but of heaven. So whenever we find ourselves in a bitter place, the remedy is not to be found in the world but rather in the spiritual. Whatever is our Father's will in heaven, let it be done on earth through us; amen. If it does not exist in heaven, perhaps it should not be part of our experience on earth, considering we are citizens of heaven. Of course, that includes sin, poverty, and sickness.

Thank you for letting me wander down that path for a moment. Now back to the task at hand. Many times in my life I have come to a crossroads and known that God was meeting me there. He would give me a correction, a direction, or a course of action, and it would always be punctuated with a promise. If I did, he would. That is exactly what happened to the Israelites at the bitter waters. Just as at the bitter waters when the answer for the Israelites was found in a chunk of wood (the cross), all the answers for us can be found not in the world but rather in the life, death, and resurrection of Jesus Christ.

Three days earlier, God had delivered the Israelites from bondage, rescued them from a trap, and destroyed their enemy by the use of an extraordinary miracle, yet when confronted with a dilemma and placed in an uncomfortable situation, they grumbled. How often do we grumble and whine about the situation instead of asking for the deliverance that the life, death, and resurrection has already secured?

Just as surely as the Lord at the bitter water "issued a ruling and instruction for the Israelites and put them to the test," he does the same for us today in order to lead us from the bondage of the world to the freedom of the kingdom. He said to them, "If you listen carefully to the Lord your God and do what is right in his eyes, if you pay attention to his commands and keep all his decrees," he will fulfill a promise. It's worth noting here that the Ten Commandments did not yet exist, nor did any of the many laws that were handed down later. Considering that, the above Scripture seems to be asking two things of the Israelites: listen to God and do what he says on a daily basis. No other commandments existed. He then went on to make them a fantastic promise. He said if they would listen and obey, he would "not bring on you any of the diseases I brought on the Egyptians."

It is much the same for us today. He asks very little of us, but generally speaking we get lost in the *if you's*. We pay so much attention to what we perceive it takes to please God that we never quite get around to claiming the promises. I'm going to tell you something now that is very important to our God growth: he is a minimum God. He does not require the maximum from us; Jesus already has fulfilled that requirement. It is simply a common-sense minimum effort that he is asking of us. In fact, he has simplified it down to two things. **"'Love the Lord your God with all your heart and with all your soul and with all your mind.' This is the first and greatest commandment. And the second is like it: 'Love your neighbor as yourself.' All the Law and the Prophets hang on these two commandments" (Matthew 22:37–40).**

I am willing to bet that you got lost in the last Scripture, wondering if you love God with all of your heart and with all of your soul and with all of your mind, and what it means if you don't. First of all, let me point out something. If God is asking you to do that, it is something he has already done. Know that he loves you with all of his heart, with all of his soul, and with all of his mind. He is not asking you for some extraordinary, superhuman, completely devoted effort. He is simply saying, Pay attention to me and I will give you life abundant. Then pass that life abundant on to those around you. I really don't care whether you think I'm taking license with the Scripture here or not, because I'm explaining to you the character of a God we can all trust. Basically, the Scripture above says that God is on our side. He is a forgiving, trusting, and encouraging God who expects us to be the same with our neighbor. This love he is speaking about is not the mushy, syrupy, marshmallow type of love we normally associate with Christianity. This love he speaks of is truthful, bold, and straightforward. It is a kind but honest discourse with our God and neighbor. It is willing to gently speak perceived truth to our neighbor. It is also willing to receive constructive correction from both God and our neighbor.

Romans 12:9 says, "Love must be sincere. Hate what is evil; cling to what is good."

Ephesians 4:15 says, "Instead, speaking the truth in love, we will in all things grow up into him who is the Head, that is, Christ." This is part of the Scripture that is telling us God has given us people to help us grow into a mature church. Implied, but not necessarily stated is that we are part of that people to bring this church to maturity, and the above Scripture is the key. Remember that small group of eight to twelve people we talked about. That is where this truth can begin in our lives and where we learn what is of the Holy Spirit and what is of our flesh.

To sum up what I'm trying to say here, let's move on from the "if you's" and begin to consider the promises. Simply said, do you know what it takes to please God? What pleases God more than anything else is for us to believe his promises. Let me ask you a question: do you like to be believed? I think it is a universal desire to be believed. How would it make us feel if we promised somebody something and they looked at us and said, "I cannot believe you"? Or equally as bad, they went their way and did actions contrary to receiving the promises? Isn't this much the same as we do to God when he makes us a promise and we simply cannot or will not believe it? Are we not, in a sense, calling God a liar? Is God speaking to us through the Bible, and does it mean what it says? And if it does not mean what it says, then what parts of it can we believe? There is a saying that goes something like, "I am not hurt because you lied to me; I am hurt because I may never be able to trust you again." If the Bible does not tell the truth 100 percent all of the time, then none of it can be trusted, including the parts about the cross and salvation. What do we consider faith to be if not simply believing his Word? **"Does God give you his Spirit and work miracles among you because you observe the law, or because you believe what you heard?" (Galatians 3:15).**

Years ago, Norma and I went to several healing crusades and
conferences put on by the leading faith healers of the day. I was
appalled by the whole charade, but particularly by the fact that the
auditoriums were made up primarily of Christians. They seemed
to be there for two reasons. They were looking for either a physical
healing or an emotionally charged experience. I do not believe either
of those things is a legitimate Christian experience. My wife and I
had at least brought with us a non-believer who needed healing.
Carnal emotion is a lie and leads us nowhere except to seek more
carnal emotion. Like a drug addiction, we need a greater high each
time, never really finding the staple, healing Jesus.

There seems to be in every crusade a desperation for God. Whether
they wanted a healing touch or an experience of something, people
seemed desperate. He is near us, as it tells us **in Romans 10:6–8:**

> **But the righteousness that is by faith says: "Do
> not say in your heart, 'Who will ascend into
> heaven?'" (that is, to bring Christ down) or
> 'Who will descend into the deep?'" (that is,
> to bring Christ up from the dead). But what
> does it say? "The word is near you; it is in your
> mouth and in your heart," that is, the word of
> faith we are proclaiming.**

I realize I've taken the above Scripture out of context; however, it
works here just as well. We do not need a preacher to bring Christ
to us through emotional hype. He is a personality who loves time
with us, and all we need to do is open our mouths, speak to him,
and believe he will speak back.

Probably even worse, though, is the need for physical healing. I have
already said that I do not believe illness—particularly major illness—
should be part of the Christian experience. I absolutely do not believe

we should be running off to a snake oil salesman to get relief from illness. I do not believe the word in James that tells us to seek out the elders is concerning itself with the physical illness. However, if we were to have physical illnesses, that would be the place to go. Let me clarify here that I do believe there is a gift of healing, but I do not believe it is for the saved; rather, it is a sign for unbelievers.

I find plenty of scriptural evidence that we are not to be sick but none more convincing than **Exodus 15:26: "I will not bring on you any of the diseases I brought on the Egyptians, for I am the Lord, who heals you."** When God said, "I am the Lord who heals you," he didn't make a statement; he identified himself. This concept is a little hard to explain, and maybe I need some help from one of the classics. In the movie *Cars,* Lightning McQueen before a race repeats to himself, "I am speed, I am speed." His attitude is that speed is not something he does; it is who he is. This is exactly what God is doing when he says, "I am the Lord who heals you." The Hebrew word is *YHWH-Rapha,* translated "I Am Who Heals" or "I Am Health." Healing is not what he does; it is who he is. This description of who God is appears more than sixty times in the Word.

Two of the Scriptures are two of my favorites. One is **Psalm 103:2–3: "Praise the Lord, O my soul and forget not all his benefits—who forgives all your sin and heals** [Rapha] **all your diseases." The second is Isaiah 61:1: "The Spirit of the Sovereign Lord is on me, because the Lord has anointed me to preach good news to the poor He has sent me to bind up** [Rapha] **the brokenhearted."**

In this chapter I have leaned heavily on the Exodus Scripture, but to really understand it, perhaps we need to be a little more analytical. Even when we are only slightly analytical, this Scripture doesn't make sense. I have found that when I look at a Scripture and it contradicts itself, God is trying to tell me something deeper. **"He** said, 'If you listen carefully to the voice of the Lord your God and do what is right in his eyes, if you pay attention to his commands and keep all his decrees, I will not bring on you any of the diseases I brought on the Egyptians, for I am the Lord, who heals you'" (Exodus 15:26). This passage has no less than four *if you's,* each of them having a different meaning from the other, and are in themselves a book, but most interesting is that they are preceded by a warning. God said, **"This is a test."** The Hebrew word for *test* can be interpreted as a moving from one level to another through the process of testing. I believe what God was saying to the Israelites is "Pay attention, for I am going to give you a 'do-over.'" That is something God does for all of us. If we have been in a certain situation and not handled it very well, oftentimes we will get an opportunity in the near future to be in a similar situation and handle it better. To put it differently, if we flunked the test the first time, we can retake it. This is exactly what happened to the Israelites. Two chapters later they are again without water. Remember, God tests our hearts, not our actions, for he knows our actions will follow our hearts. In Exodus 15, God was telling the Israelites to change their hearts so that the next time they were thirsty, their actions would be different. Unfortunately, they did not heed the warning, and their actions in chapter 17 were more abominable than in chapter 15.

Right about here is where verse 26 begins to be confusing. God says that if we do the *if you's,* he will not put any of the diseases of the Egyptians (the world) on us. Then he says, "For I am the God who heals." I don't need healing if I don't have any disease. Therein lies my dilemma: if I'm good, I won't have any disease, and if I don't have any disease, I don't need healing. So what is God really saying here? When I asked him, this is what I heard: **"Enter through the narrow gate. For wide is the gate and broad is the road that leads to destruction, and many enter through it. But small is the gate and narrow the road that leads to life, and only a**

few find it" (Matthew 7:13–14). Well, there you see, that made things clear as mud.

As I continue the conversation with God, he showed me a narrow path leading into infinity and said, "This is the road that I am upon, and as you stay close enough to me to hear me speak to you, you are on this path with me, and then all of the I am's are yours." I would not say that I was less confused now, but I did know He was taking me somewhere that I really wanted to go. I said, "I am not sure what the four *if you's* have to do with the I am's." His answer surprised me, but then, he is the God of surprises.

He said, "The four *if you's* are the tools of a shepherd. They are equivalent to the rod, the staff, the voice, and the presence. When you know that you are protected by my rod and rescued by my staff, when you listen to my voice and stand in my presence, then I am your 'I am.' Then I am your Jehovah-Raah (The Lord My Shepherd), and as you allow me to shepherd you, I will become all of your I am's. You will have no need of anything, for I will be your Jehovah Jireh (The Lord Will Provide), you will have no sickness for I will be your Jehovah Rapha (The Lord That Heals), and you will stand holy before me because I will be your Jehovah Mekoddishkem (The Lord Who Sanctifies You).

Suddenly I realized what God was saying to me. It is not that we will be healthy, prosperous, and holy as a reward because we are good girls and boys when we obey him; rather, when we obey him, we are one with him, and when we are one with him, we cannot be sick, poor, or sinful, for he is health, prosperity, and holiness. Jesus expresses this in **John 14:10: "Don't you believe that I am in the Father, and that the Father is in me? The words I say to you are not just my own.** *Rather, it is the Father, living in me, who is doing his work"* **(emphasis mine).**

Most of all we want to make sure that we are not the people of **Jude 1:5: "Though you already know all this, I want to remind you that the Lord delivered his people out of Egypt, but later destroyed those who did not believe."** Rather, we want to be the people of **Hebrews 10:39: "But we are not of those who shrink back and are destroyed, but of those who believe and are saved."**

Why, when James without doubt says, "God will raise him up," does it sound just confident, but when I say it, it sounds presumptuous and perhaps even arrogant? Presumptuous and arrogant or not, I will make two statements. If you go to the elders and they pray and you are not healed, the problem is not with God, and the answer is not with the doctors.

CHAPTER 24

Wear Good Shoes

This volume is not intended to add to the endless words about who God is, what he wants, and what our purpose is. Our goal is to as simply as possible use the Word of God to show that through Jesus Christ, the Father has provided us with all things (2 Corinthians 9:8), and our purpose is to simply believe the unbelievable. And even this believing is not of ourselves but is a gift from him (Hebrews 12:2). So consider this: if Jesus is the author and perfecter of our faith (that is our belief), then the only thing that would keep us from receiving all his promises is our choice not to believe.

If I do not have any credibility left with you at all, I understand. The above is a purpose statement of this book from chapter 1. I believe I have completely failed that statement, and 60,000 words later, I am still going. I do not believe I have brought any simplicity to the matter whatsoever. But there is hope. I have almost reached the end. In this chapter I want to scripturally make the case that the health and well-being of our bodies is the responsibility of Jesus Christ, and after that, almost as a contradiction, I want to stress some things we can do to enjoy life to the fullest. As I sit before the computer screen, I have been quite sick for several days (see the chapter called "My Ordeal") and have completely rededicated the health of my body and the life I have as God's responsibility. I am not the first person to advocate faith-based health over the medical community. There are many others, such as John A. Dowie. I have noticed that our normal outlook on medicine is such a stronghold of the Devil that those who come against it often come under severe attack.

As we look at Scriptures, there is little doubt that we are part of the body of Christ. **Romans 12:4–5** says, **"Just as each of us has one body with many members, and these members do not all have the same function, so in Christ we who are many form one body, and each member belongs to all the others." First Corinthians 12:27** says, **"Now you are the body of Christ, and each one of you is a part of it."** And **First Corinthians 10:17** says, **"Because there is one loaf, we, who are many, are one body, for we all partake of the one loaf."**

But as I began to look at Ephesians 5:25–33, the theory put forth in this Scripture also applied to God's care for us and his responsibility to us as both our intended husband and as the head of our body:

> **Husbands, love your wives, just as Christ loved the church and gave himself up for her to make her holy, cleansing her by the washing with water through the word, and to present her to himself as a radiant church, without stain or wrinkle or any other blemish, but holy and blameless. In this same way, husbands ought to love their wives as their own bodies. He who loves his wife loves himself. After all, no one ever hated his own body, but he feeds and cares for it, just as Christ does the church—for we are members of his body. "For this reason a man will leave his father and mother and be united to his wife, and the two will become one flesh." This is a profound mystery—but I am talking about Christ and the church. However,**

each one of you also must love his wife as he loves himself, and the wife must respect her husband. (Ephesians 5:25–33)

The above is an extremely comprehensive piece of Scripture. It deals with relationships between husbands and wives, Christ and his church, an individual and his body, and ultimately, I believe, Christ and the individual. But for my purposes here ,I am most interested in **verse 29: "After all, no one ever hated his own body, but he feeds and cares for it."** I believe we can find a principle of God relating to his people in this verse. It is well established that we are his body, and the above Scripture says that someone feeds and cares for his body. The words *feeds and cares for* would be used to talk about a shepherd caring for his flocks. He is responsible for their nourishment, safety, and health. I personally prefer the words some other translations use, such as *cherish* and *nurture*. These words more accurately describe the relationship between a parent and child, particularly a mother and her baby. Looking at the Scripture is why I believe that if we allow him, God is ultimately responsible for our complete well-being in body, soul, and spirit. I think the above Scripture makes him responsible, for on the one hand, he directs people to feed and care for their bodies, and in the same passage of Scripture, he declares we are his body.

Now, with that said and readily admitting I will sound like a hypocrite, I think there are certain things we can and should do to give our bodies an easy path in the kingdom. It seems to me the two statements are in opposition to each other, and I admit that I believe God's care for us trumps anything we can do. I also admit my hypocrisy in making these suggestions, because I am overweight, eat red meat, salt my food, and do very little of the things I'm suggesting.

I made a list of the common things that the world says we should do to remain healthy, and in doing so, I noticed that it had many similarities with the list associated with controlling our blood pressure. In reviewing these lists, I came to the conclusion that number one for helping our bodies function at the optimum performance level is controlling our blood pressure. Hypertension or high blood pressure is called the silent killer and robs us of energy, feelings of well-being, and victory in life. When I speak of controlling one's blood pressure, I don't mean running to the doctor and getting a pill. Rather, I mean controlling our weight (we are an overweight nation), controlling our sodium intake, eating healthfully (including lots of fruits and vegetables), eating less red meat, and getting aerobic exercise daily. My son, who had high blood pressure and was on medication for it, decided to lose weight. He dropped twenty pounds and began exercising. One day we were working on a project and he simply did not have anywhere near his usual get-up-and-go. Besides being lethargic, he was sweating and complaining that he didn't feel good. Come to find out his blood pressure was quite low, and the doctor suggested that if he lost twenty more pounds, he might not need medicine at all. Another toll taker on the human body is stress. We are a society driven to succeed, and climbing the ladder of success generally means that the higher we go, the rarer the atmosphere and the more stress we experience. I have spoken in the past of the segmentation of the crucifixion, and I am convinced that the crown of thorns placed upon Christ's head is our remedy for stress. The mind is the source of worry that creates stress, and the crown of thorns encircles the mind. **"The one who received the seed that fell among the thorns is the man who hears the word, but the worries of this life and the deceitfulness of wealth choke it, making it unfruitful" (Matthew 13:22).**

I realize the title of this chapter sounds a little unusual, but it originates from an actual experience in my life. Most of my life I have done heavy physical work, and I never experienced back problems. Suddenly several months ago I noticed my back ached in the evenings. I wondered why, even in my prayers. One day I felt an urge to look at the bottoms of my work shoes. I noticed that the heels on both shoes were quite worn, although the leather uppers were in good shape. At this point I must mention that I am, in my words, quite frugal, and in my wife's words, cheap. Looking down at my shoes it had never occurred to me that they were worn out. I went that day and bought a new pair, and that was the end of my back distress. So wear good shoes, and in the same vein, have a good mattress and get plenty of rest.

In vain you rise early
and stay up late,
toiling for food to eat—
for he grants sleep to those he loves. (Psalm 127:2)

Drink lots of water and not much alcohol. Brush your teeth and keep all other good hygiene practices.

Okay, I realize this chapter is sounding a little secular. Please do not misunderstand me: I'm not in the least bit suggesting that without doing the above suggestions, we cannot be healthy. I truly believe the only one who can completely care for our health and well-being is Jesus Christ. However, the suggestions I made would be good for our health and definitely good for our discipline. **"No discipline seems pleasant at the time, but painful. Later on, however, it produces a harvest of righteousness and peace for those who have been trained by it" (Hebrews 12:11).** If we were to review the "to do" above, we could easily see that several if not most of the things require discipline. If we look at the Scripture above, we see that discipline develops righteousness and peace. I think we would also be hard-pressed not to admit that the above suggestions would also be good for our bodies. This would make us double winners if we were to just apply the discipline.

However, I have one more suggestion that I have recently been made aware of that I believe will also benefit our spirits. While shopping at one of our local thrift stores, my wife came across a DVD by Joseph Prince called *Receiving Healing with Faith and Patience.* The DVD ministered to the entire fellowship, but one part particularly ministered to me. In the DVD, Joseph mentions taking Communion on a daily basis, and I have personally found this to be a refreshing and healing experience. Jesus said, "Do this in remembrance of me," and when I do it, I remember all he gave up to provide me with salvation: his spirit, health, holiness, and prosperity by allowing his body to be beaten and crucified and his blood to be shed.

CHAPTER 25

That's All, Folks

Praise the Lord, O my soul,
and forget not all his benefits—
who forgives all your sins
and heals all your diseases,
who redeems your life from the pit
and crowns you with love and compassion,
who satisfies your desires with good things
so that your youth is renewed like the eagle's.
—Psalm 103:2–5

Generally speaking, I rely heavily upon New Testament Scriptures, but if I were to believe there was a signature Bible passage for this book, it would be the one above. I think at the beginning of writing this book, my intent was simply to remind us not to forget his benefits. But not long into this process, I began to realize the absolute comprehensive concern and care he has devoted to us, and I further realized that this was a much bigger undertaking than I first thought. I realized that this care is so pervasive in his character, so needed by us, his people, and so inclusive of every area of our being, that it would be nearly impossible to include every benefit individually.

At this point I felt the Holy Spirit ask me, "What are the basic needs of every human being?" Then he showed how God's promises fulfill them. Of course, salvation and the infilling of his Holy Spirit were paramount among our needs, but three others almost immediately came to mind.

Answering that question many months ago is what led to the compiling of this manuscript. As I have said several times, I believe there are three things humans need to live life abundantly. Each of us needs to find esteem for self, and when properly understood, holiness gives us this. For we know the truth of **Romans 7:18**, which says, **"I know that nothing good lives in me, that is, in my sinful nature."** This esteem for self can be found only in the holiness of Jesus Christ, which he has freely given us. A case can be made—although in my opinion a pathetic one—that sickness brings us to a higher, more holy place and therefore is God's will for us. Take it from someone who was recently sick: it is definitely not the abundant life. God's promise of health is the abundant life, along with his promises to give us everything we need to live that life.

I do not necessarily understand why these promises, which are so clearly expressed in his Word, remain so elusive in our experience. I do, however, understand where they originate. They originate in the love of God: **"For God so loved the world that he gave his one and only Son" (John 3:16); and "But because of his great love for us, God, who is rich in mercy, made us alive with Christ even when we were dead in transgressions" (Ephesians 2:4).** Many men throughout history have sacrificed their sons. Some have even killed them because they were a threat. There are also legends about Greek gods sacrificing their sons, so to ancients this was not a preposterous thought and did not actually drive the point home, because they could not understand a God of love.

What the Scriptures actually say is that God is a God of love, and that to kill, particularly the one he loved the most, was so foreign to him that it could have destroyed who he was. Rather, it was a statement of the depth of feeling he has toward us and what he was willing to risk to bring us to him. **First John 3:1** says, **"How great is the love the Father has lavished on us, that we should be called children of God!" And that is what we are!** Civilization at the time of Christ could imagine a man or even a God killing his child, but they could not imagine a God who loved so much that he would call ordinary men his children, for that would make them equal to him, and a threat.

This extraordinary, unconventional love is what the hearts of men desired and what made Christianity so extraordinarily different from other religions: a God of love who interacted with those he loved. I believe even today the reason we miss out on the abundance of God's blessing in our lives and the reason we don't appropriate his promises is that we underestimate this incomparable love the Father has for us.

Ephesians 3:17–19 says, **"And I pray that you, being rooted and established in love, may have power, together with all the saints, to grasp how wide and long and high and deep is the love of Christ, and to know this love that surpasses knowledge."** This Scripture is somewhat of an oxymoron, for it encourages us to know this love of God and in the same sentence tells us this love cannot be known, for it surpasses knowledge. This is another reason that Christianity thrived from the beginning. It simply was not just an intellectual experience; it was beyond intellect, and it was also the Holy Spirit touching our emotion. If the knowledge of this love surpassed knowledge, the only way we can receive it is by an impartation of the Holy Spirit. This is equally true today.

I call the above Scripture my cubic Scripture. It talks about the width, the length, the height, and the depth of Christ's love, which makes this love cubic. Imagine it as a box around you that extends from the ground to eternity on all four sides and is filled with his love. Every breath you take is a breath of God. This knowledge is why Paul could exclaim in **Romans 8:38–39, "For I am convinced that neither death nor life, neither angels nor demons, neither the present nor the future, nor any powers, neither height nor depth, nor anything else in all creation, will be able to separate us from the love of God that is in Christ Jesus our Lord."** The love of God that is in Jesus Christ is one that desires for us to live an abundant life. The only one thing that can keep us from living the abundant life is believing the lie.

The worst lie of all is dispensationalism, or rather, the use of dispensationalism as an excuse to dismiss certain phenomena today because they do not fit into our religious doctrine. If it is in the Word of God in the New Testament, it is as good today as it was a couple of thousand years ago. **John 10:35** tells us that—**"Scripture cannot be set aside."**

We all have an identity crisis. We identify with the earthly man and fail to recognize the heavenly man. We live in the defeat of the earthly man and fail to grasp the victory of the heavenly man.

"His divine power has given us everything we need for life and godliness through our knowledge of him who called us by his own glory and goodness. *Through these he has given us his very great and precious promises, so that through them you may participate in the divine nature* **and escape the corruption in the world caused by evil desires"** (2 Peter 1:3–9, emphasis mine).

God is a personal God and tells us we can have our needs met by simply referring to the names he uses to describe who he is. For instance, if we need provision (prosperity), we simply need to call on Yahweh-Jireh, "The Lord Will Provide"; if we need healing, we can say the name Yahweh-Rapha, "The Lord Who Heals"; and if there is an area in our life we are struggling to overcome, we can simply call on Yahweh-M'Kaddesh, "The Lord Who Sanctifies, Makes Holy."

Yahweh-Jireh, "The Lord Will Provide," in Genesis 22:14, is the name memorialized by Abraham when God provided the ram to be sacrificed in place of Isaac.

Yahweh-Rapha, "The Lord Who Heals," is from Exodus 15:26, which says, "I am Jehovah who heals you" both in body and soul. He heals us in body by preserving us from and curing diseases, and heals us in soul by pardoning our iniquities.

Yahweh-M'Kaddesh means "The Lord Who Sanctifies, Makes Holy." In Leviticus 20:8 and Ezekiel 37:28, God makes it clear that he alone, not the law, can cleanse his people and make them holy.

I come from and have contributed to a politically motivated family. We are capitalists, individualists, pro-life, pro–traditional family, and Christian. Something else that we are after the last few years is frustrated. The benefit of this frustration is that it has led to several discussions, primarily with my son-in-law, who has spent time in Europe and is a student of history. These discussions have led me to some simple conclusions. The world already has a one-world government. It has had since the fall of Adam and Eve, and until the new one-world government takes over, the first will reign. Let me explain! The Devil is the God of this world, and no matter how many forms of government we have, he ultimately runs them all. This world is an evil theocracy, and until the kingdom of God comes in its fullness, establishing a righteous theocracy, this world will remain evil.

I have been asked, "What does it matter?" I could give a religious answer and say, "Because if I work hard for righteousness, it will bring forth righteousness quicker." Or I could say, "I want to see as many people saved into the kingdom of God as I can." Either one of those answers would not be anything other than self-serving. The real answer is that I so enjoy life on the fringes of the kingdom of

God, and so believe the world I presently live in provides the most and best opportunity for that life to continue, that I have worked in the past to preserve that form of life.

I have come to realize that maybe this form of life must die before I can fully enter into the kingdom of God. This is a prospect that I meet with both anxiety (perhaps honestly called fear) and anticipation. The reason for the anxiety should be obvious—evil must become stronger before love triumphs—but the anticipation is truly an honest emotion. The little of the kingdom of God that I have tasted is so sweet that it is hard for me to imagine the fullness thereof.

"Above all else, guard your heart, for it is the wellspring of life" (Proverbs 4:23).